Pearls on a String

One Woman's Journey to the Past

MARTHA ANDREA AAS

X-presso
books

Cover and interior design by Tony Dierckins
Cover art and map on page 60-61 by Tony Dierckins

All photos contained herein are from the author's private collection.

First Edition, 2007

07 08 09 10 11 • 5 4 3 2 1

Library of Congress Control Number: 2007923797

Softcover ISBNs: 1-887317-78-3 & 978-1-887317-78-8

Printed in U.S.A.

Contact the author at:
maas@cpinternet.com

Published by the author with the help of

Duluth, Minnesota, USA • www.x-communication.org

In loving memory of my parents
Marius Anders and Eleanora Kristine Borch-Jensen,
my sister Elin Eisler, and my brother Johannes Borch-Jensen

— M.A.A.

———————

Thanks go to my sister Frida Borum and to my late sister
Anna Galustian for claiming their memories while
helping me remember mine;

to Milan Kovacovich for urging me to write;

to Paulette Bates Alden for her
encouragement as teacher, mentor, and friend;

to my friends in the Lake Superior Writers' memoir writing group:
Kay Coventry, Jeanice Fontaine, Destri Irwin, Margaret Kinetz,
Dorothy Lutz, Donna Schilling, and Shirley Wuchter
for their invaluable critiques of my work;

to Mara Kirk Hart for her steady support;

to my children, Peter Aas and Christine Aas-Larsen, for proofreading
the manuscript;

and not least to my husband Johannes Aas for his loving acceptance
of my absent-mindedness and preoccupation while in writing.

— M.A.A.

Contents

Looking Back • 1981

Roots • 2002

Prologue

I descended from the plane and walked across the tarmac into the dark African night. The hot, muggy air hit my face and made my clothes stick to my body. I took a deep breath inhaling the sultry air that carried on it the smell of smoke: the smell of millions of outdoor kitchen fires, the smell of burning twigs and branches cut from immature trees, the smell of fires lit between three rocks on which rest the pots of *Ndolé*, the smell of Africa.

The mugginess and the sickening smoke imparted a sense of danger that immediately put me on edge. I had thought myself immune to all assaults now in my middle age, yet I knew that the relative wealth my white skin signified made me a target here. I walked through a long hall whose louvered glass windows were broken or absent and passed through vaccination and passport checkpoints. Surly officials appeared to relish the opportunity to pounce on any irregularity or mistake, often to pave the way for extracting bribes.

One of our bags containing medical supplies was missing. In the glass-enclosed cubicle housing the Lost and Found, two clerks sat at either side of a mammoth desk facing early model computers. An inefficient air-conditioner droned in the background. Tired from the long flight, I was about to lose my patience as the clerk slowly and with great gravity entered my information into the computer. I wondered if the computer connected to an international luggage network that could track my bag. Mostly likely not, I thought, and I expected never to see it again.

Outside on the curb, waiting for the van that was to take my husband and me to the hotel, a young porter spoke to me in French:

"So you will have a new president tomorrow, a president elected by fraud."

I was non-committal:

"Well, do we really know that?"

"Ah, *mais bien sûr*! The United States has now become like Africa."

In January of 2001, I was in Cameroon for the third time to continue the medical exchange program my husband and I had conceived of in 1997 and started in 1999. The program had grown exponentially and was now an NGO (non-profit non-governmental organization), which managed its limited resources well and had been able to effect significant changes in the health system of the Lutheran Church of Cameroon.

Douala was a rundown former French colonial seaport. The grand four-lane highway leading into town was sparsely lit; we descended as if into a black hole. The chauffeur of the hotel van drove too fast and narrowly missed a broken-down truck blocking the right lane. Listing colonial buildings with wide, shady verandas marked the beginning of the town, the walls around their compounds crumbling. Despite its pretentiousness, the highway had many potholes; the city streets had even more.

Again, this country overwhelmed me with its many reminders of my childhood, of a colonial era long gone. I was sixty-four years old, yet I felt fourteen as Douala took me back fifty years: back to another French colonial seaport, Djibouti, and back to the British Crown Colony of Aden on the opposite Arabian coast. I had moved to Aden when I was twelve years old. My Danish parents were missionaries there. For thirty-six years, they preached the gospel—unsuccessfully by many people's standards—to the uniformly Islamic population.

Old and new friends, people from the hospital and the African church community, met us when we arrived at our destination the next day. The welcome we two doctors received was warm and overwhelming. We traveled in a cortege through town, dodging potholes, dodging garbage.

Arriving at the church compound, a former mission station, we were shown to our accommodations, a house with shiny cement floors, polished by many years of wash and wear, with louvered, screened windows, and with sparse, functional furniture. In all its simplicity, the house reminded me of my childhood home in Aden. Yet, the kitchen with its gleaming white, modern appliances was nothing like my mother's primitive kitchen of fifty years before. I again saw my mother, Eleanor, standing by the kerosene stove in the small, hot, dimly lit kitchen, clad in a thin cotton dress, sweat pouring from her brow as she prepared the family's dinners, the kerosene-powered refrigerator in the corner enveloping her in hot fumes.

We had arrived in Ngaoundéré, Cameroon in the dry season, during the coolest time of year. The sun had scorched the ground and gone was the lush grass I remembered from my first stay here. Flame trees spread a translucent canopy of green leaves and flaming red flowers that contrasted vividly with the forget-me-not blues of the jacarandas. Red clay had turned to red dust, dust covered everything. The mango tree's shiny leaves were no longer green but gray; only the new shoots projected like dark red showers at the top, dotted with spikes of pale green flowers. Dust covered all surfaces inside as well: the slatted windows were opaque, the kitchen counter pink. How much like Aden, I thought, there the dust had been equally pervasive.

We unpacked the small amount of clothing we had brought and the generous medical supplies we had spent our last weeks before departure collecting. To our surprise, we received a message that our lost bag was found, was in Paris, and would be forwarded to us.

On our way to dinner at a short-term missionary's house, we ran into an older missionary couple who had spent a lifetime here. Sam had just come from a church council meeting.

"After forty years I thought I knew these people, but I have no clue what the secretary tried to say with his backhanded remarks," he said in his high-pitched, plaintive voice. "Oh, well, soon I am retiring to the States and of course there I shall also be an outsider and I will probably not understand my fellow Americans either," he added. His wife talked with enthusiasm about the young man walking with them:

"Pierre loves Jesus! I just know he does." All I needed to do was to close my eyes to hear my mother speaking, the same lilt to the voice, the same conviction. Inger wore the same type of shapeless dress my mother used to wear. Her blond hair had turned gray. If she had pulled her hair back in a bun, the resemblance would have been complete. I felt the missionary daughter stirring in me; yet it seemed as if I was now walking in my mother's shoes. I felt a confusion of emotions: anger and irritation at the patronizing, puerile praise bestowed on the native Christian, but also admiration for the couple's dedication to this their life's work, amazement at their sacrifices, and great empathy for their sense of dislocation; long forgotten, intensely familiar emotions. This was like a homecoming.

From 1927 to 1963, my parents, Marius and Eleanor, natives of Denmark, had been missionaries in Aden, Yemen, then the British Crown Colony of Aden in Southern Arabia. For thirty-six years they had preached the gospel of Christ, for thirty-six years, they had sacrificed themselves and their family to God's work, for thirty-six years—save the years of home leave—they had lived among Muslims. Like the missionaries in Cameroon, they devoted their lives to God. I think of their determined struggle. I know how hard their lives were though their dedication and conviction often prevented them from seeing it that way. I spent my early teen-age years in Aden; the war and my mother's home stays had kept me in Denmark until age twelve. I was of a cognizant age then and everything I experienced left a strong imprint on me. Those years were luminescent and though I felt confined, Aden to me was a beautiful and exotic world. Coming of age there had been somewhat disconcerting.

For years, I had wanted to revisit my childhood home in Aden, but continued political turmoil in the region had made that impossible. After the British had left in 1967, the protectorate of Aden became South Yemen. It turned Communist and closed its borders to the West in the years it received support from the Soviet Union. With the fall of the latter, however, communism soon became outdated, but civil war with North Yemen then followed, the region became unstable, and remained inaccessible. In 1994, the North and the South had reunited to become the Republic of Yemen, stability returned, and I took heart hoping now to be able to visit Aden soon. The new state opened its doors, and fascinated tourists from Europe flocked to a country that in its interior had remained untouched and medieval. However, disenfranchised tribes in remote areas soon took to kidnapping tourists as a way of exerting pressure on the central government to meet their demands for improved services, new roads, and other perceived needs. The kidnap-pings happened with increasing frequency and Yemen became a risky tourist destination. I saw my hopes dashed all over. Then on October 12, 2000, one of Osama bin Laden's cells blew a hole in the American warship the *U.S.S. Cole* in Aden Harbor—one in a string of terrorist attacks on U.S. property abroad—and I knew that as an American I might never feel safe in Yemen.

I had visited Yemen's neighbor, the progressive country of Oman, in 1999. The trip was a teaser and intended as a prelude to a visit to Yemen. In Oman's far corners the culture and the language of the people were very similar to those of the Yemenites, and I found my Arabic come rushing back; the more I talked the more long forgotten words came tripping across my lips. The culmination of the visit came one day when I stood in the moun-tains of southern Oman, gazing across the border into Yemen, as if into a promised land. Frustration filled me at the tantalizing proximity of a country I could not visit.

Now in Cameroon in 2001 I rethought my wish to revisit my childhood home. So many things had changed. In the desert of Oman, I had visited a Bedouin family's tent. In it were a television set and a gas stove. They had replaced the black home-woven tent covering, whose color blended so well with the desert, with an incongruous blue plastic tarp. The family's young son served coffee, not from the customary decorated silver coffee pot, but from a thermos. The Bedouin, though displaying great pride in his camels, also owned a pick-up truck.

For me, the Arabia I had known, and which until recently had not changed since medieval times, was gone. Maybe I did not want to see Yemen the way it was now, especially Aden where the civil war had left profound marks. Maybe I just wanted to remember it the way it was fifty years before. I was not yet prepared to confront the changes in Yemen. I did not want my memories tainted; I wanted to keep them intact.

My father, Marius, had kept diaries from about nineteen-seventeen until the nineteen-thirties. These diaries formed the basis for memoirs he later took the time to write and copies of which he sent to his children. I had brought them with me to Cameroon on my first visit in 1997 and had spent my evenings translating my father's memoirs from Danish to English for my grandchildren. Later that year, after returning to my home in Duluth, Minnesota and inspired by these memoirs, I began writing about my own past.

It was not until this third visit to Cameroon, however, that I realized that only by exploring my parents' past could I place my own in the right context.

On my return to Minnesota in 2001, I began patching together the fabric of my parents' lives. My father's memoirs became a treasure trove for me. They revealed aspects of my parents lives with which I was not familiar and emphasized others I already knew. The books my father had written about their missionary work became another resource. They revealed the joys and many of the difficulties they experienced in trying to win the Arabs for the Gospel.

In my attempt to understand my parents, I was faced with a myriad of questions. They had come out of peasant and working class Danish stock. Why had they not followed the path of their forebears? What set them apart? What moved them to take the turn in the road and follow a call to serve God in such an audacious manner?

Many believe themselves called to serve God. Osama bin Laden's terrorists are convinced they do God's will, but their purpose is evil and destructive and some would have the same sentiments about the Christian Crusaders and the Spanish Inquisitors. I, however, saw only good intentions in my parents' work. Yet as I grew older, I often questioned my religion's command to Christianize the world and my parents' specific mission to bring Christianity to the Muslims. I found much nobility in other religions and was inclined to religious tolerance; but I had learned to admire my parents' commitment to their cause and their tenacity. I felt separated from them, however. They lived in a world I could no longer inhabit or understand and for which I had ambivalent feelings. A barrier had been erected between us. What had gone awry along the way for that to happen? Was their Christianity too confining, their commitment to God too consuming? Was their work more important to them than their children were? Yet why, I wondered, was I now doing humanitarian work in a third world country, following their example to some degree?

What follows here is my attempt at seeking answers. It should be obvious to the reader that what I tell of my parents is my—the author's—perception of the persons they were; the scenes in their lives are based on knowledge I have gleaned from their memoirs as well as on events that I remember. These are facts, not fiction. I have however created some scenes, not from actual memory of them, but from the knowledge of events that make such scenes likely.

❸

Childhood

(1937–1950)

A Woman of Valor

*It was called "Arabia Eudaemon" [Arabia Felix] and it was
formerly a city, when the voyage was not yet made from India to
Egypt, and when they did not dare to sail from Egypt to the ports
across this [Indian] Ocean, but all came together at this place;
in those days it used to receive the cargoes from both countries...."*
— THE PERIPLUS OF THE ERYTHRAEAN SEA, 1ST CENTURY A.D.

I was conceived in the town of Crater in the British Crown Colony of
Aden; in what was of old known as *Arabia Felix*—Arabia the Joyous. I was
due at the height of summer, a treacherous time of year. Hence my parents
made the prudent decision that my mother would deliver in Denmark.

So when in mid May 1937 the P&O liner steamed out of Aden, onboard
would be my pregnant mother Eleanor and four-year-old Elin. My father Marius and Frida and Johannes—eight and six—would follow a month later.

At the time, my parents lived in a colonial house at Front Bay, in the
town prosaically called Crater as it lay in an extinguished volcano. The peninsula of Aden, curving like a C around the Bay of Aden—the harbor—con-
sisted of bare, towering volcanic rock, sand, azure waters, and blinding white
houses. Its searing light and heat must have caused my mother to yearn for
the muted color and coolness of Denmark.

She had first come here thirteen years before and was now forty years old.
In my mind's eye I can see her: short and plump, her dark blond hair gathered in
a bun, she must have moved with difficulty in her pregnant state. I imagine her
surroundings whose shimmering light and fluttering dust devils indicated that
the monsoon season had arrived. Palm trees, their trunks curving, swung in the

steady breeze. Heat, sand, ocean salt, goats, camels, and exotic scents created a sensual background for the multitude of nationals living here. During the day Hindi and Arab women passed by the old colonial house on their way to the market, the former dressed in colorful saris, the latter in black chadors. In the evening voluble Hindi and Pakistani men and Arabs dressed in long futas (sarongs), loose shirts and turbans ambled past on their daily walk to the beach.

My mother loved Aden. Did she know as she said goodbye in 1937 that she would not return for another twelve years?

I can also easily imagine my three siblings here. They spent many afternoons at the seaside with their ayah, Qaha. As my sister and I did years later, they must often have walked across the causeway to Sira Island, the old Turkish fortress, stopping on the way to watch the eddies of water between the island and the main land. There the waves crashed, green and frothy, scouring the rocks and recoiling in giddy laughter, like a horde of adolescents unaware of their strength. Colorful fish maneuvered through the roiling waters and darted in and out of caves carved by the surge. This was a place to watch the fish, not to swim. Like us, our siblings swam with the British colonials at Gold Mohur or *Gulmohur* (the Hindi for Flame Tree), a beach club, whose enclosures kept out sharks and non-whites.

Once before my mother had left Aden precipitously. My parents' first child, Frida, had been born in March of 1929 in the midst of a smallpox epidemic. Scores of people had succumbed to the illness; covered from head to toe with crusty sheets of blood-tinged yellow pustules, blood gushing from their mouths and guts, they had died.

My parents quickly vaccinated Frida and moved with her to "The House by the Sea," as they called it. The house lay on top of the volcanic hills with a view of the ocean; there the dangerous vapors of the city could not reach her, they thought; there she was protected. Yet, she did not thrive and when she gained only three pounds in as many months, my mother fled Aden with her in May of 1929.

Aden has variously been called a hellhole and the most beautiful of cities. Since it is the only natural harbor on the part of the Arabian coastline bordering on the Red Sea and the Indian Ocean, it has a long history as a seaport and had probably been active as early as 440 B.C. Kingdoms had come and gone in Southern Arabia, and each had wanted Aden as their sea-port. Destruction had attended every transfer of power, yet Aden remained an important port-of-call on the way to India. When Vasco da Gama discovered an alternate route to India, Aden declined in importance only to re-emerge as a transit port after the Suez Canal was built. By then the East India Company had conquered it and made it a coaling station, placing it under the administration of the British Raj in India. In 1937 Aden became a British Crown colony directly under Britain and subsequently it played an important role as a British air and naval base during WWII. Through the British Empire's Divide and Rule Policy, the area surrounding Aden came under British protection. Treaties were signed with the tribes and the area became known as the British Protectorate of Aden.

Let me pause here to express my wonder at how my mother, a poor, small-town, working-class girl from Denmark, came to find herself in Arabia.

Her father worked at the railroads, at a job that provided a pension, but little money. Both she and her two brothers left school at age fourteen to support themselves. My mother often expressed regret about this; she would have liked to continue school and later she would be driven to give her children the best education possible.

Yet like all girls of working-class background she had been forced to find a job as a maid, where she could learn housekeeping and mark time until she married. At age eighteen—appropriately—she had found a railroad man to whom she became engaged.

During this time my grandmother became caught up in the revival movement sweeping the country, and my mother often went with her to meetings. Later, as my mother would tell it, she had, at nineteen, attended a large Lenten revival meeting and had come to faith in Jesus. It was difficult for her to accept God's call, but she had been unable to ignore it.

Some years later, she had felt God calling her to preach the gospel to the heathens. Eventually, as she attended meetings by missionaries from Arabia, the Call became more focused: God wanted her in Arabia. The young railroad man did not understand this and with sadness she broke off the engagement.

She had applied to the Danish Arab Mission, which informed her that to become a missionary she would need a profession. Diligently she set aside money, and by age twenty-five she was able to start a Pre-School Teacher's education in Copenhagen. Those were for her exciting and difficult years. She worked, went to school, and studied at night. She never knew where the money would come from, but the Lord provided, and often when she had not a penny left, money arrived in the mail from an anonymous supporter. Then she had gone to England to learn English and had worked in the London slums and finally, when she was twenty-eight, she had been ready to leave for Arabia.

Now this is what I find so remarkable. My mother was an ordinary woman whose sights—one might have expected—would have been set on marriage to a person of equal or higher social standing and raising a family. One would not have anticipated she would travel the world, and certainly not alone. First she set off for England to learn a new language, a remarkable feat for someone with her limited linguistic abilities. Then she set out on her own for the deserts of Arabia, an accepted romantic destination for dashing young Englishmen such as Lawrence of Arabia, but not necessarily for a single, Danish pre-school teacher. It was as if she threw all caution aside, or as she would have said: God guided her.

She traveled by train to Genoa in Italy. There she stayed for several days at the local YWCA waiting for her ship. In Genoa she made an excursion alone to the famed cemetery, Campo Sancto; became lost; could ask directions from no one as people spoke only Italian; thought herself doomed to wander the streets of Genoa forever when finally she happened upon a woman who spoke Swedish, her mother's tongue, and got safely back to the Y. Thereafter my aquaphobic, non-swimming mother, ventured onto a freighter bound for Aden. What trust!

She arrived there in 1924 without having gone to language school; the Mission had indicated she was needed immediately. This was somewhat discouraging, as she thought there was little she could do without knowing Arabic. But she found her mission in helping the other missionaries by keeping house for them, and by teaching sewing and physical education in the Mission's Girls' School.

The next year, in 1925, she was finally off to language school in Syria where, a year later, she would meet my father.

Courtship

My parents met in 1926 in a part of Syria that is now part of the state of Lebanon. Both were fledgling missionaries studying Arabic, she in Syria, he in Egypt.

My father had come to Cairo from Denmark in November of 1925 and had studied at the School of Oriental Studies at the American University. My father and mother knew of each other as they were employed by the same mission society, and though they had never met, they corresponded.

When the summer of 1926 came, though he could barely afford it, my father decided to leave the heat of Egypt to travel to Syria where it was cooler. He traveled steerage on a freighter where a friendly Syrian took pity on him and shared his blanket and food with him.

My parents' first meeting was at the Hôtel Métropol in Beirut where my mother had arranged to meet my father. She dined with him and then she saw him off to Brumana in the mountains east of Beirut, not far from Shimlan where she herself was vacationing.

She had liked my father so much that she paid him a surprise visit two weeks later, and together they made an excursion into Beirut. My mother offered to arrange lodging for him at Shimlan, a nicer place, she suggested; besides that was where all the missionaries congregated, she told him, and he accepted.

In Shimlan they studied Arabic and Islam together and played tennis in the evening with other missionaries. They were a group of many nationalities, and on weekends, they all went on outings together. The Mediterranean was a favorite destination.

My father vividly remembered one particular trip there, a story he often told us. They arrived at the beach in two cars. Some brought deck chairs; others spread their blankets on the rocky beach. The sun reflected off the water, and the women squinted against the light, not being able to keep it out of their eyes despite their wide-brimmed hats that the wind threatened to carry away. The afternoon was hot and blustery, and there was a surf. My father loved the water and he loved to swim. Despite words of caution, and probably believing himself invincible, he threw himself into the surf and basked in the warm Mediterranean water. He swam and swam, far from shore. Finally, when he turned around, he found himself struggling to get back. He almost depleted his strength before reaching land, staggered onto the beach, and collapsed. My father loved to challenge himself, but later he acknowledged his foolishness. He became remorseful and said he felt he had tested God's patience. He was destined to do God's work. How could he have been so arrogant as to risk his life?

In Shimlan my parents took to sitting outside on a rocky promontory close to their lodgings, reading together. My mother offered to darn my father's socks and he gratefully accepted. While she sat on a blanket nearby working on his socks my father read aloud, elbows on knees, open book in hand.

Then Miss Andersen, the older woman missionary from Aden who was vacationing in the same place, took my father aside and told him to either make some declaration of intent or stop seeing so much of my mother. This forced my father to make a decision. He asked my mother to marry him after having known her for only two months. She accepted. My father wrote in his diary: We prayed for God's blessing, prayed that we would grow in love and grace, that God would guide us in our future separations and times together, and that His Love would shine on our work, our hardships, our joys, and sorrows.

Yet my father was also concerned that they were so unlike; he worried they might be incompatible. Maybe I'll bore her. Am I too quiet? I don't talk much, he wrote in his diary. Does she talk too much? he asked himself; sometimes it seems she just chatters away mindlessly. He also knew about himself that he often brooded or pondered things deeply without being able to communicate his thoughts.

Yet a year later on September 7, while on vacation from the heat of Aden, they were married at the British Legation in Addis Ababa in what was then called Abyssinia (now Ethiopia).

The Adventurer

Being a missionary was never for the faint-of-heart. So how had life prepared my father—a lean man of medium height, with a balding pate, prominent blue eyes, and a moustache—for this?

He had grown up in poverty. Every May to October from age seven, he lodged with a farmer who gave him board, lodging, and clothing while he herded the farmer's cows. At fourteen he left school to work as a day laborer on farms. This was hard work where he often lived in crowded quarters and where nutrition was poor. Consequently, at age twenty, pale and malnourished, he was admitted to a sanatorium with tuberculosis. Having long known that he wanted further education, he had saved toward the goal of becoming an engineer and when at the end of four months in the sanatorium he was much improved—in fact apparently healed since he never again had further signs of TB—he began preparing himself for his engineering studies.

Shortly thereafter he became convinced, however, that God had other plans for him. He left his studies to enter a six-year *diakon* (deacon) apprenticeship at Kolonien Filadelfia, a Christian institution caring for chronically ill epileptics. The *diakon* in medieval times was a philanthropic servant of the church. In Denmark in the early twentieth century deacons were educated to minister to both the soul and body of the sick and elderly. This was a profession that suited my father well; he was a compassionate man.

Though he grew up in abject poverty he came out of an illustrious Danish family, the family Borch of Jutland, whose ancestry can be traced back to the sixteenth century, to the first professor of anatomy at the University of Copenhagen in Denmark, Ole Worm. A physician, runologist (one who studies runes), and archeologist Ole Worm was the Renaissance man I am sure my father would have wanted to be. My father was an autodidact who taught himself shoe repairing, book binding, German, English and some Latin, and though non-musical he taught himself to read music and play hymns on the organ; all were skills that stood him in good stead as an emissary of God with few means.

His family had belonged to the peasantry for only two generations. His great-grandfather, Frederik, an upright Christian man, owned *Skjern Hovedgaard* (Skjern Manor House) in Jutland with land holdings of about 700 acres, not a negligible acreage even at that time. Here he raised eight sons most of whom—that is to say all but Erhard, the oldest, my father's grandfather—had higher education and eventually became prominent citizens in Denmark. A brain injury in childhood (measles encephalitis it was speculated) had affected Erhard's intellect as well as his temperament. He had little schooling and as a young man he worked for farmers. He attracted his father's displeasure when he fell in love with the housekeeper Marie and Frederik sent them their separate ways: Marie to give birth to my grandmother under rather dismal conditions, Erhard to his uncle's farm. The two young people eventually managed to marry without Frederik's consent. Later Frederik relented somewhat, bought them a small house—not far from the manor—and secured a job for Erhard as a *vejmand* (a road repair man). The 19th century Danish poet Jeppe Aakjær wrote a much-loved song about the *vejmand* ("*Hvem sidder der bag skærmen…*") set to music by Carl Nielsen, describing him in pitiful terms. Erhard struggled to support his wife and children, notwithstanding surreptitious help from his mother, and the next generation, among them my grandmother and her family, remained very poor.

When my father finished his deacon's training, God called him to serve in Arabia, a call that he heeded unquestioningly. My mother's brothers often teased my father saying he became a missionary for one reason only: to fulfill his love of adventure. Though there was a kernel of truth therein—my father indeed loved adventure—he foremost burned with a passion to spread the word of God. Did adventures for him take off the sting of disappointment when his evangelizing efforts failed? Maybe.

One thing was sure however: his love of adventure was intricately linked to his love of story telling. When in 1929 my mother had gone back to Denmark alone with Frida, my father remained behind to finish up his term. During the summer of 1929 he vacationed in Ethiopia and his experiences there gave rise to stories often told.

He had taken the boat as usual from Aden to Djibouti, and the train from Djibouti to Dire-Dawa in Ethiopia. During the last leg of the journey—a ride on mule-back from Dire-Dawa to Harrar—something happened, the meaning of which my father long pondered.

He set out with the mule-driver guide early in the morning. All day they trekked across the mountains where a detour due to flooding took them past their lunch-stop. My father was hungry, exhausted, and hoping they would soon be at their destination when he came across a woman lying face down on the path. He figured she had been out begging for food—they had a famine in the area—and that she had fallen over from hunger and exhaustion. The local peasants paid her no attention; they were in a great hurry to get their cattle home because night was falling and the hyenas would soon be out.

My father stops, turns her over, and when he finds that she is unconscious he decides not to leave her there. My slim, but strong father picks her up, places her across his mule, and supports her while the mule-driver leads his mule onward. They arrive at a village where my father hopes someone will take her in, but the women outside the huts wave their hands at him, as if to tell him not to approach. He approaches nonetheless, and since he doesn't know the language he communicates through signing; they finally allow him to sit the woman up against a hut. He gives them money and signs to them that they must feed her and give her something to drink. He does not want to leave the woman there, but if he takes her with him, it will take so much longer to get to Harrar and she may die before they arrive. On the other hand, he isn't sure the women at the hut will do as he asks. Maybe they'll just leave the woman to die; she isn't of their tribe, so they don't feel responsible for her. Yet he leaves her, intending to go back for her with a physician and better transportation.

When they arrive at the Swedish Mission station in Harrar after dark, he realizes his rescue mission will have to wait for daylight, and then he wakes the next morning with a high fever, is delirious and sick in bed for a week. No one goes back for the woman. In the end nothing comes of his good intentions.

My father often expressed his distress about this outcome of his intended rescue mission. He had not fulfilled the role in which he had cast himself as the Good Samaritan. He fretted over it, tried to convince himself that he could have done nothing more, but it was no consolation. For a time he had been convinced he had failed God. Surely, God had wanted him to be the Good Samaritan. But later he wondered. Maybe God had other plans. Maybe being a Good Samaritan was a role my father had created for himself, and not what God wanted. In the end he concluded that he had not been attentive enough to what God wanted him to do.

Subsequently, however, he had his full measure of adventure. He hunted lions with the Swedish missionaries in Harrar, and in Addis Ababa, an English Colonel invited him to his farm. He and the colonel set out on horseback. On their way there, my father related, they encountered swollen rivers that the horses swam across while he and the colonel crossed crawling on all fours on bridging tree-trunks. He envied the colonel his large colonial farm; my father loved to grow things. The colonel had many kinds of grain on his land, and his dairy cattle produced butter he sold in the city. He also had strawberries and raspberries, and deep in a valley into which plunged a tributary to the Nile, he had an orchard. He invited my father to help him plant new fruit trees there. To get to the orchard they had to crawl backwards down the steep mountainside; they worked there until the sun became too harsh forcing them to find shelter. My father placed himself in the opening of a cave, where he sat reading, writing, and taking in the full measure of the large fruitful valley. At the end of the day, mules carried them out of the ravine. My father blithely spent a week with the farmer.

In 1930 my parents were reunited, but this would only be the first of many times they were separated.

A Troubling Separation

I was born at the end of July in 1937. My parents expected a boy and wanted to name him Andreas for my father's brother who had drowned when he was ten. When I turned out to be a girl, they instead choose the name Martha Andrea.

I have often looked at the picture of my paternal grandmother, Erhardine (or "Dine" as she was called), and her five children taken just before Andreas's drowning. Andreas was a beautiful, blond haired boy with a wide forehead and large inquisitive blue eyes. My grandmother had lost her husband just before this picture was taken and was soon to lose her ten-year-old boy: how could one survive such losses? Letters between my grandmother and my father attest to the love and affection they felt for each other. She was a strong and loving woman. She died at age seventy just a few weeks after my father came to Cairo in 1926; he was disturbed that he had been unable to be with her on her deathbed.

My father and older siblings arrived in Aarhus, Denmark, before my birth. By then we had moved into an apartment in the center of town not far from my maternal grandparents. The apartment was an old patrician flat with stucco-ceilings. It was on the third floor and had two large rooms toward the front, a big kitchen, and a small bedroom in the back. My mother wanted me to be outside sleeping in my pram every day; fresh air was good for children and gave them rosy cheeks, she said. She placed the pram in the backyard where she could keep an eye on it from the kitchen window.

During this time my parents came to the realization that it was wisest that my father go back to Aden alone. My mother knew it was in the best interest of the children that she stayed with them in Denmark. Frida and Johs needed to be in school, as would soon Elin. More important, however, was the political situation in Europe. Hitler in his fiery, loud speeches talked about *Lebensraum* for the Germans. The situation was getting tense. If war broke out, my parents and the whole family would remain in Aden for the duration of the war, and no one knew how long that would be. It would be easier for my father to make his way back alone if it came to war. Fortunately, the mission had agreed that he would only be gone for two years.

They found a cheaper, newer apartment and moved there before my father left. The apartment was nice and light, but it was small. The three older children slept in the bedroom, my mother and I in the living room. A maid helped my mother with house chores and made it possible for her to go out occasionally. She saw her parents and brother and sister-in-law every Sunday when we went there for dinner. Yet no doubt she must have felt very lonely.

At three months I contracted whooping cough. I went through spells of coughing for weeks on end where no cough medicine helped. I seemed to fight for every breath and at times it must have been difficult for me to nurse. I slept next to my mother in the sofa sleeper. Whenever I went into severe coughing spells my mother picked me up and walked the floors with me. I am sure my mother missed my father during those times. However she has often said that I was a great support to her during those years and when I was younger I often wondered how that could have been. My own children showed me how an undemanding and cuddly baby can be a great comfort to hold.

Then a letter from my father turned my mother's world upside down. It was 1938 and he wrote her about a trip he undertook to the independent state of Yemen, to its capital Sana'a. The Imam of Yemen had allowed medical missionaries into the country and my father went there to see if some of the Danish nurses could work there. To that end, he traveled north by car with one of the Danish nurses. Apparently, he felt very attracted to her and admitted to himself the wrongness of his feelings, yet felt compelled to confess them to my mother; after all, they did not keep anything from each other.

My mother became consumed by jealousy. I can imagine the thoughts she might have had: How could he be attracted to someone else? Did he not love her anymore? And as doubts assailed her I imagine her writing him long letters railing at him. How could he feel that way about another woman? Not that he had acted on his feelings, but God looked at what was in men's hearts, she might have said, and it was a sin to covet someone other than your wife. She must have felt unwanted and inadequate, caught in the doldrums of caring single-handedly for four children. My mother had no one to share this with; she certainly would have told neither her parents nor her brothers. She definitely would not have admitted to them that there were problems in her marriage. She would have wanted them to believe that she had the perfect marriage.

It is hard today to imagine how completely separated my parents were. They could communicate only via airmail: no phone contact, no e-mail, none of the forms of communication that today can bring friends and relatives from across the world right into our living rooms. Needless to say—it might also have been desirable had my father not felt the need to be so brutally honest.

Yet my mother survived the two years and finally she was able to look forward to the day when my father was back. Her spirits rose in anticipation and she talked to me about my father, who I did not remember, showing me his picture. She wanted me to know him: "This is your Daddy, Martha, and he is coming back to us soon."

My father arrived at the end of May of 1939 just a few months before the Germans invaded Sudetenland. The day he arrived my older siblings ran right into his arms, and after a moment's hesitation I followed suit.

When my mother put me to bed that night, it was in a cot in the bedroom. She told me that I must now sleep with my siblings. "Dad will sleep next to me in the living-room."

I cried myself to sleep that night.

Vivid Memories

Memories are stored in many parts of the brain and are believed to be processed in the hippocampus. In the process of retrieval, memories may be "colored" and may have a different quality once they are again stored. Repeated examining can thus "color" a memory permanently. Retelling of incidents from childhood by parents also leave such an imprint in a child's brain that the child—now adult—may insert itself into the memory of a sibling believing unequivocally that the event happened to her while the older sibling knows this cannot be true.

My memories of my early childhood are few, but vivid. Clearly, in most of my memories I remember things that only I could have known about, and I therefore know they are my memories. Others have been fashioned out of stories repeatedly told where I am reputed—or believe myself—to be the person in the memory. However through reading other people's stories and hearing siblings retell memories, I know that memory is faulty and that I may be wrong about some of my memories. But I will retell them exactly as I found them when I recently retrieved them from where they are stored in my brain.

I am playing on the sidewalk outside the apartment building where we lived from my birth until I was six. I am about two years old. My few toys are lying around me. I am in a harness, the leash of which is tied to the railing of the basement stairs. I can move as far as the leash is long, which allows me to approach the curb.

I have been told that the man who rented our attic room—the theology student, Moses—at times would bring me up to my mother when he found me bored on the sidewalk. He untied me, picked me up by the waist, set me on his shoulders, and carried me up the stairs. He was tall and had to bend to ease me under the doorframe. I was on the sidewalk because my mother believed that fresh air kept a child healthy. Meanwhile she attended to chores in the apartment.

My mother was a concerned mother, and an early childhood education teacher. Neither ignorance nor neglect induced her to place me, her two-year-old, on the sidewalk to play by myself. At that time the community helped protect children; nobody conceived that anyone would abduct a child. Other mothers placed their children outside in like fashion. The harness was to keep the child safe; yet, looking back, I shudder when I think of what harm I could have come to because of the harness and the railing.

I am in my stroller. The man I have recently been told is my father has lined us up on the sidewalk. Frida stands behind the stroller and Johs hangs on to it. Elin stands independently on the other side. We are on the way to the beach.

These trips to the beach were frequent during the summer; four children were difficult to contain within a one-bedroom apartment. My father had just returned from Aden and I had not seen him since I was a newborn.

"Cheese," Dad says in English. My siblings smile, but I am too busy attending to my bonnet.

My father loved swimming and water. I am sure that he let me splash as much as I wanted once we arrived at the beach and let me dunk my head until I coughed and sputtered.

Later he takes a picture of me on the beach. Again, he says cheese, and again I am tentative, not knowing whether I should smile at him.

On the back of the sepia colored picture my father has written "brown as an Arab."

I am in an apartment across the street. I see my father at his small, dark desk where he wrote his sermons and where he wrote numbers in a little black book. The budget was tight; his wartime salary of 500 kroner did not go far. The desk is behind the window of our living room. He closes the book carefully around the red and black numbers and places it in a drawer. Behind the window, I also see hanging the large red Hudson Bay woolen blanket that covered our window at night. Its purpose was dual. It was our blackout and it kept the room warm during the cold winter-nights of the war.

I am about four years old. I am playing in the basement with other children from the apartment building. We chase each other down the hallways, from one room to the other, dodging under clothes hanging in the drying room. The wet sheets swish across our faces. An older boy tells us to take off our clothes. Hooting and shouting we continue to run through the basement. I sense that my parents will be displeased with me running around nude and I know I should not mention this.

I go to nursery school a block away, in an old patrician villa. I go there alone. A tall hedge surrounds the garden. I open the wire-fenced gate, walk down a path with flowerbeds on both sides, to a door at the side of the villa. The room inside the door is full of small open cubicles. I hang my coat, undo the ankle straps of my clogs, and put on my slippers. Some days when it rains the room smells of damp wool.

Our toys are wooden trains and trucks, and dolls with squishy bodies; their arms, legs, and heads pop like ping-pong balls. Sometimes the skins of their bodies break and I pull out handfuls of kapok. We paint with watercolors on rough unbleached paper, *karduspapir*. Our lunch is *mælkebrød*, rye bread in milk. The brown bread becomes gooey and sticky in the warm milk; I feel sick to my stomach.

There are *kolonihaver* across the road from the nursery school, allotment gardens for people who live in apartments—little tiny plots where they grow vegetables and fruits. They build small houses with one or two tiny rooms and a kitchen. They build them from whatever material they can appropriate. And around every little plot is a hedge, and every tiny lawn has a flagpole that flies the *Dannebrog*—the Danish flag. There is a law, my father says, that the flag must come down at sundown. Everyone carefully lowers the flag at the same time. These houses are like dolls' houses and I wish my family had one.

I like to watch what goes on in the allotment gardens. People sing, play, plant, harvest, laugh, and cry, and all the while they drink coffee. Every afternoon they drink coffee and have *wienerbrød*(Danish pastry). I envy them. My parents never give us wienerbrød. It is too expensive and not healthy, they say. I imagine that the people in the allotment gardens must be rich, they have wienerbrød all the time, and strawberries with cream and sugar!

I wish we could have pastry just once in a while.

Trapped in Denmark

I don't know what my mother was doing in town that day. She could have been shopping—not that there was much to shop for in 1944—or she could have paid a visit to Dr. Aggebo at the other end of town. There could have been any number of reasons for her being out and about.

By this time, Denmark was well into its fourth year of German occupation. Germany had invaded Denmark in 1940 and with only a force of 15,000 the country had capitulated peacefully, fulfilling Winston Churchill's words of February 1940: "I could not reproach Denmark if she surrendered to Nazi attack. The other two Scandinavian countries, Norway and Sweden, have at least a ditch over which they can feed the tiger, but Denmark is so terribly near to Germany...."

So when Germany had invaded Norway and Denmark on April 9 the Danes had surrendered while the Norwegians had not. Both peoples had been ferocious Vikings, but the Danes had settled into being peaceful and moderate and had realized they could not possibly withstand the German force without much unnecessary bloodshed. Before the invasion they had cringed in the shadow of the German Reich trying not to provoke their mighty neighbor and hoping to stay out of the war, they had declared their neutrality. But now that the Germans were inside their borders, had there been any other option but to surrender?

As my mother made her way through town that day, she may have passed the Hotel Royal on *Store Torv* (Big Square). Through windows framed by lace curtains, she could have seen German officers dining at tables covered

with gleaming white tablecloths and drinking out of crystal glasses filled with
expensive wines. The Germans had taken over the hotel ensuring their officers the best accommodations in town. I imagine her seething with anger:
they enjoyed themselves while their troops inflicted misery on the world. Like
everyone else, my mother wanted the Germans out of her country, and she
wanted the war to be over.

The Germans had promised the Danish Government independence and the
two governments between them initially adopted a policy of negotiation; as
far as the Germans were concerned Denmark was the perfect Aryan State that
also could provide Germany with agricultural and industrial products; as long
as the Danes cooperated, life would continue as before. This was a promise
not kept. Almost immediately the Germans curtailed the press and soon other
civil liberties were eroded. The resistance was slow in developing, but increasingly resistance members sabotaged German rail transports and German instal-
lations; an underground press kept the populace informed. When the Danish
government finally refused to cooperate anymore, the Germans in August of
1943 disbanded the government, army, and navy and imposed martial law.

As she proceeded through town, my mother would have crossed *Lille Torv*
(Little Square) and continued into *Guldsmedgade* (Goldsmith Alley). This
was a narrow street where a truck passing on the outside of a tram could
almost block the traffic. Wartime trucks used wood-burning generators that
emitted choking black smoke. Most often there wasn't much traffic here; no
private cars were on the road and her brother Anker's roadster now sat on
blocks in his garage. There was rationing of most consumer goods. Gas was
available, but only to the Germans.

My parents were trapped in Denmark by the war. There was no possibility
of traveling to Aden as the borders were closed now. Our family had grown
with the addition of my sister Anna Margrethe who was born exactly one
month prior to the German invasion on March 9, 1940. Now a family of
seven we had in 1943 moved out of the one-bedroom apartment and into
a newly built house with a garden in which my father grew all our own
produce, as his salary barely sustained us. For my mother thrift was a way

of life. Our family's survival depended on it. With the help of a seamstress, she remade clothes donated to us. Her meals were starchy but filling, and occasionally farmers who supported our parents' mission gave us meat. In summer vegetables and fruits from the garden nourished us and in winter my mother supplemented our meals with cod liver oil.

> Had the sirens sounded that day, my mother would have hurried to the bunker in *Vennelyst Park* and run down its concrete steps. The allies had formerly bombed during the night only, but now they also flew surveillance and bombing raids during the day. She would have sat on the concrete bench with people around her that all had had their day disrupted, yet took it in stride. Some women had their knitting with them; having unraveled their old woolen sweaters they were now knitting new sweaters for their children and grandchildren. Some of the people around her would have had their shoes filled with newspapers; leather for new soles was hard to come by.

My father was at home more now, though he continued to have meetings around the country. He had traveled by train at the beginning of the war, but now that trains had been appropriated for German troop transports, he traveled everywhere on bike. He enjoyed biking, he said; he could think and prepare his sermons on the bike. My father was obsessed with fitness; no matter where he was he did his calisthenics every morning without fail and took a cold shower. We saw him take off on his bike, dressed in tweed plus fours, shirt, tie, and jacket and with a sixpence on his head, his bag with his clothes and papers on the bike-carrier. When he arrived home, he rang the bike bell persistently until we heard him and ran out to welcome him back. We worried what might happen to him when he was out. Could the Germans find some reason to detain him? A lost identification card? A mistaken identity?

> And then, as my mother continued on her way, toward her on the sidewalk came two German soldiers, young men talking animatedly between themselves, laughing. I imagine my mother as she walked along, not raising her eyes to them, looking straight at the pavement, but just as they were about to pass her, she quickly lifted her face and spat on them. Astounded, the soldiers let her continue on her way.

❂

Allied Bombings

I was in class at the private school, *Fru Laursens Realskole*, where my mother finally sent me when I reached second grade; I was seven years old. My mother had home-schooled me until then and I had been content to learn at her side.

That morning I was busy doing sums. Carefully I lined up the numbers on the squared paper. Looking out the window I saw a dreary, gray sky, with the clouds hanging low over the old apartment buildings across the street.

It was October 31, 1944, a day that would prove to be like no other.

Although I, as a three to six-year-old, had been unaware of what had happened from the time of occupation and until the Germans imposed martial law, I was aware that the son of family friends was a Freedom Fighter who eventually went underground. I also vaguely remember the *Frit Danmark* underground paper my parents received. Wartime events for me became like photographic negatives brought into focus by postwar happenings. After the war my classmate, Annie Blatt returned from Sweden. Her father was a professor at Aarhus University and as Jews, her family had been evacuated during the war. Only much later did I learn about what had happened to the Danish Jews.

From the first days of the occupation the Danes had supported the Danish Jews; most were native Danes who had come to Denmark three hundred years before. In the spirit of the policy of negotiations the Germans had initially adopted a soft approach toward the Jews. However when sabotage and uprisings led to the state of emergency, the Germans finally in October 1943 decided to round up the Jews. But news of this got out and, spreading by word-of-mouth within a day, almost every Jew in Denmark was warned and enabled to seek shelter with non-Jews; therefore when the Germans raided Jewish homes only about 300 Jews were taken. Subsequently the resistance organized the escape of approximately 7,000 Danish Jews to Sweden, a non-occupied country. After the war these actions would be resoundingly lauded throughout the world.

A sudden whistling and a boom tore through the air. Boom followed boom in rapid succession. The teacher put down her math book:

"Stop what you are doing. Pick up your satchels and line up in two rows. Take your coats in the hall and follow me to the bomb shelter."

Everything happened so fast. We were drilled for this; we knew we had to hurry. We always returned from the playground in two rows and now as the sirens whined, we quickly found our places and hurried after the teacher.

Curfews and blackouts were part of daily life for me, something that only became clear to me when after the war I saw bright lights shining from windows. Rationing was also part of life, and of course we had no exotic imports like oranges and bananas, but an after-war memory is of eating an orange at Christmas for the first time—oh, the wonder of it.

Soon we were in the basement shelter with the rest of the students from the school. As we crouched on the benches, we continued to hear the whistling of the bombs before they exploded. Everything was so close. What were the British bombing? Could they be bombing the German camp next to our family's house? I wondered. I was sure that my parents and four-year-old Anna were now in our basement shelter.

That shelter became quite familiar to us as war ground on. At night, as soon as the sirens sounded, we always scurried out of bed drunken with sleep, running down the two flights of stairs to the room against whose windows my father had stacked sandbags. We stayed there during the emergency alarms, and the snapping of the anti-aircraft guns from the German camp next door tended to keep us awake. We huddled in makeshift beds and sometimes we stayed there all night. At other times, we went back upstairs when the alarms sounded off, but then the sirens often came on again with a new attack, and back down we went. Late in the war my parents could not get Frida and Johs out of bed; tired of getting their sleep disrupted they ignored our parents, turned over and went back to sleep.

In the school's shelter we continued to hear the throbbing sounds of Allied planes. It was ominous how one could hear the planes very faintly in the distance, and then the sound grew and grew until it was at its loudest and one knew the planes were close, and wondered what was going to happen. Now the sound of the planes grew to an almost continuous dense buzzing, reaching a slight climax just before the bombs exploded. It was not the camp, I decided. The planes were much too loud. It must be somewhere closer.

After a while we heard no more bombing and the sirens blew off the alarm. Everyone got ready to go back to class, but the principal stopped us.

"I am sending you all home. I want you to pair up, girl with boy, and be on your way."

I was paired with Klaus who lived just a block from my house.

"Now stay together. Hold each other's hand, and run or walk as quickly as you can."

Klaus and I had a two-mile walk ahead of us. I took his hand once we were out in the schoolyard. There I noticed that everyone was staring in the same direction, toward a dust cloud.

"The apartment building. It must have been hit."

One wall was still standing with half a floor attached to it, the wall-paper torn.

"A missed target?" I thought as I caught a glimpse of a group of people, maybe the occupants of the flats, staring grief stricken at the destruction; the apartment building had almost collapsed. Klaus and I ran down the street to-ward *Nørregade*, up along *Vennelyst Park* to *Kirkegårdsvej*—the Cemetery Road that separated two large cemeteries. Then we slowed to a walk. I let go of his hand; everything was quiet.

Just then, the sirens sounded again and people started running past us, hoping to get to the bunkers up ahead, but the planes were almost upon us and we all threw ourselves on the ground. I clung to Klaus's hand as I pressed myself against the sidewalk. Whatever they might be bombing, I hoped they didn't miss their target again. The bombs whizzed through the air and exploded with such intensity that I felt my eardrums quiver. I pushed myself hard against the ground as if to leave my imprint there. I had no time for fear; I thought only of the moment, as my surroundings exploded in noise. As flames and smoke rose into the sky beyond the trees on my left, an acrid smell of explosives drifted across us.

After an eternity, it was all over. The silence was crushing, but we got up and ran. When again we reached streets with apartment complexes, we sought the backyards, not wanting to be out in the open, but we heard no more planes, no more bombings, just silence. Finally, we felt it safe to take the shortest route home and after another fifteen minutes we were in our suburban neighborhood. Klaus and I separated one block from my street, and I rushed home.

My older sisters and my brother were still at school. My parents seemed quite relaxed however and I thought they must know that everything was fine. The four of us sat around the kitchen table for lunch. My father talked about how he had seen the British planes duck into the backyard almost right outside the kitchen window to avoid the anti-aircraft fire from the German camp.

"I could clearly see the British pilot," he said, as if relating another great adventure.

Later while reading *The Bitter Years: The Invasion and Occupation of Denmark and Norway* I learned what had happened: Three squadrons of Mosquito bombers, each consisting of six planes, had skimmed across the North Sea from Scotland at an altitude of approximately fifty feet. They had climbed slightly as the coast of Jutland rose ahead of them, and then they had leveled off to continue their tree trimming flight towards Aarhus. Low clouds had hung over the city that day. The planes had come in beneath the cloud cover and had achieved complete surprise, not a shot was fired as the first wave made its bombing run. The Gestapo Headquarters at Aarhus University was completely destroyed and with it many Germans and some Danish prisoners and informants.

What Was I Thinking?

I was lying under the barbed wire fence. I knew the guard made his rounds about once an hour, so I thought I could get under the fence and through the surrounding trees and bushes to see what was going on inside the camp. I was here on a dare; my friends waited for me outside the fence. Now I was under—and carefully I crawled through the bushes, around the trees, and out into the open. There had been soccer fields here before the Germans took over the Stadium, but I was too young then to remember that. What I saw before me were barracks upon wooden barracks that stretched all the way to the Club House.

It was now the summer of 1947 and the war was over. On the eve of May 5, 1945, we had heard over the BBC that the German High Command had surrendered all German forces in Denmark. I remember the evening clearly. Though I was already in bed I got up and sat on the upstairs landing to watch the goings-on. My father hung a huge Danish flag from the second floor balcony; Frida and Johs rushed into town to participate in the celebrations in the streets; in panic frightened German soldiers who knew nothing about the surrender opened fire and people were wounded; my siblings were unhurt. In celebration of the liberation families one by one lit candles in their windows and soon the entire country lit up. Since then, each year on May 5th Danes light candles and place them in their windows.

German soldiers were interned in the camp next door. I had always thought them intimidating, but once the war was over, they all looked a little lost; all they wanted was to go home. My friends and I often went to the main entrance of the camp around which the soldiers clustered, pale and unhealthy looking, their uniforms dirty and worn, their hair unkempt. They begged us children to run errands for them, to go to the bakery for pastry, bread, anything to eat, or to run to the kiosk for cigarettes or beer. In exchange they offered helmets, uniforms, caps, even guns and cartridges and out of curiosity some children obliged them. I dared not do that. I thought with dismay of what my parents would say had I brought home a German gun. Yet, the soldiers longed to have cigarettes, to have something better than camp food, to have something sweet from the bakery, to have some of life's little luxuries. Some of them were so young, maybe no older than fourteen or fifteen. I imagine now how those young boys might just have wanted to be out in the street, or on fields back home in their villages playing soccer. I wonder if these boy-soldiers ever regained their adolescence.

> I lay quietly at the edge of the grass. It was late afternoon, but the sun was still warm. The camp was quiet. Now in 1947 the German soldiers had gone home and instead political prisoners and refugees crowded the camp. Danish soldiers guarded them.

Our house on Hans Egedesvej was one of many in rows and rows of similar houses populated with working class families. I have happy memories of summer evenings playing hopscotch with my friends on the sidewalk; walking on stilts; and playing with marbles on the not yet blacktopped street where my father during the war had collected horses' droppings with which to fertilize his garden. I also remember often being in bed by ten o'clock when it was still light and other children were still playing outside, and feeling resentment that I alone was in bed.

> I was lying here in my nice school dress. What had I been thinking? I had gotten dirt all over it and my mother was going to be upset with me. I really completely disliked this dress; it was uncomfortable having been made out of cellulose, a wood product, and it itched like crazy. My mother said she had been lucky to obtain many meters of it and the seamstress had sewn dresses for us girls, but none of us had shown any enthusiasm about them. I couldn't wait until I could get new dresses, like Anni Blatt. Anni was dressed like a queen; there had been no shortages in Sweden, it seemed.

In our house on Hans Egedesvej I woke up early every morning to practice the piano before going to school. My first teacher had beat me across the knuckles with a ruler when I played wrong notes; the more she hit me the worse I played. I was quickly transferred to The People's Music School where I began lessons in piano and solfège.

> All of a sudden, I heard the guard. Here I had been thinking of my dress and not paying attention. I quickly backed up through the bushes as the guard came closer.
>
> "Stop, who is there?" He stepped between the trees. I slipped under the fence and just then, I heard my dress rip. Oh, no, I thought, I'm in trouble. My friends helped me up and we ran with the guard shouting after us.
>
> I stopped to check my dress. Sure enough, it was torn. I didn't want to go home, my mother would be furious. It was the only nice dress I had; now my mother had to darn it as nicely as possible and then not only were my socks darned, but now also my dress. I wished I had completely ruined it, so I wouldn't have to wear it anymore. That was wishful thinking: my mother could fix anything.

Our house on Hans Egedesvej had one toilet, but neither a shower nor hot water. We washed in cold water at a sink on the landing upstairs and once a week—after the laundry was done—we bathed in the laundry room, in a wooden tub filled with water from a cauldron heated with coal. When my father had been home our parents spent an entire day once a week doing all our laundry: boiling the whites in the cauldron, scrubbing dirty clothes on the washboard, rinsing them, putting them through the wringer, and hanging them outside. Doing laundry for a family of seven was an arduous task. My mother could consider herself lucky; she had my father or Bedstefar to help her, many women had only themselves. Once everything was dry my mother would iron, press, and spend hours repairing torn clothes and darning holes in socks.

> I did not want to go home, but dinnertime was approaching; I was expected. I told my mother right away, what was the point in waiting?

"You tore your dress? How could you? That nice dress."

I didn't offer any excuses.

"So how did this happen?"

I explained. My mother's face turned white, she didn't say anything for a while, but then she said:

"Let's sit down and have dinner first."

I ate my dinner in silence. I knew I was in trouble. My mother was alone with us now. My father had gone back to Aden again. At least I wouldn't have to face his wrath, I thought. My father's anger was often intense.

When dinner was over and the dishes cleared away Mum said:

"Let's go downstairs."

We went to the room with the big mangle on which all our bed linen and tablecloths were pressed. Bedstefar—my mother's father who lived with us— now helped with the mangling on washdays. He and my mother wet down linen and tablecloths, stretched and folded them, wrapped them around the mangle stick, and rolled them between the two pressing surfaces. I usually liked it here when I helped Bedstefar push the mangle, but today I would rather have been anywhere else.

My mother took out the rug beater—the one Bedstefar used outside to beat the dirt out of our rugs—and asked me to bend over the chair in the corner. She pulled my dress over my buttocks. With two hands on the rug beater she beat me as hard as she could. I didn't say a word, I knew I deserved punishment, and my mother seemed to think this was what she must do. It hurt, but I was not about to acknowledge that. I had the sense that my mother was punishing me not just to teach me a lesson, but out of fear; did she fear I could have been shot?

As I left the basement, I heard Bedstefar coming in from the garden:

"You are being too hard on the children, Nora," he said to my mother.

"They have to learn their lessons," she retorted, resenting her father's interference.

Yet I knew my mother hated to be the one to mete out discipline.

My Grandfather

Some time in 1947 Bedstefar, who was living with us, became sick with a cough and a fever. He went to bed; this was unusual for him, and my mother realized she must call the doctor.

Bedstefar had been living with us since my father's departure. After my grandmother, Alfrida, died in 1942 he lived by himself close to my uncle Anker and his family. But when my father went back to Aden in the fall of 1946, my mother knew she needed a man in the house, so her father came to live with us. We loved Bedstefar, especially Frida, and Bedstefar reciprocated her love; he had loved her since he first set eyes on her.

In 1929 when my mother had come home alone from Aden with Frida she had taken the ferry from Harwich in England to Esbjerg, and Bedstefar had met her at the dock. She had left Denmark a single woman and had returned married, and with a baby. My uncle Anker and his wife Jenny had come to Esbjerg with my grandfather and they had driven my mother, Frida, and Bedstefar back to our grandparents' home north of Aarhus. Bedstefar Mikkel had held Frida in his lap all the way, not wanting to let her go.

"Isn't it getting to be too much for you, Dad?" my mother had asked. But he was emphatic; he wanted to hold the baby. But, though Frida was tiny, my mother was sure Bedstefar arms were tired and stiff when he finally four hours later let go of her.

My mother and Frida lived with our grandparents for eight months before my father returned from Aden, and Bedstefar had been Frida's constant companion. During the first days of my father's return Bedstefar would hold Frida in his arms and ask her:

"Do you want to go to your daddy?"

When she refused and clung to him, Bedstefar was in his glory.

When my father was about to leave in 1946, my parents had decided that Johs would go to boarding school. It was too much for my mother to handle three adolescents alone. Frida was seventeen, Johs fifteen, and Elin thirteen. Johs showed little interest; he was quite content to stay at home, but he accepted the decision without fuss. Once he had left, my mother had room for her father to stay with us. He was a good support and helped her around the house with many small practical things.

Bedstefar normally started the fire every morning. I would hear him from my bed every day hauling in peat and coals and rustling out the ashes from the stove in the dining room, and as he got the fire going the warmth would spread to the rest of the house.

But the morning of his fever my mother had gotten the peat and the coals in the basement and had started the fire herself. Then after seeing the kids off to school she had gone off to call the doctor. Thank goodness, Dr. Aggebo had answered the phone and promised to be out soon.

When he arrived he shed the heavy coat with the furry lapels he always wore and went up to Bedstefar's room. Dr. Aggebo had made house calls on us from the time we were born, so I find it easy to imagine his visit.

"Well, let me check you out so I can see what's going on with you." Dr. Aggebo took out a tongue depressor, otoscope, and stethoscope and soon he was peering into Bedstefar's throat and ears, percussing and listening to his chest. He listened long and carefully, and must have been very thoughtful as he folded up his instruments and put them back in the valise.

"Mikkel, you have pneumonia and you will be quite ill for several more days until things start turning around. I can help you with that cough of yours. I will give you a cough mixture, and then I will be back to see you tomorrow again."

He was very matter-of-fact. Bedstefar would have appreciated that; he didn't like people fussing over him. My mother then followed Dr. Aggebo downstairs into the dining room where he closed the door behind her.

"His pneumonia is extensive; both sides are involved. He may not survive this, Eleanor. He is eighty-one years old. No spring chicken. I wish I had some of this new antibiotic, penicillin [penicillin was first produced in Denmark in 1947]; that would surely cure him. But I will give him some sulfa and that may also do the trick. I'll be back tomorrow." He then wrote out the prescriptions, got his coat and left.

It would have been difficult for my mother to contemplate the thought of losing Bedstefar especially at a time when my father was not there. She was unable to call my father and talk to him, we didn't have a phone, but even if we did I am not sure there was service to Aden at that time.

After Dr. Aggebo left she would have taken her bike and biked to the pharmacy in Trøjborg. There in a dim, quiet hall pharmacists in white lab coats stood at the mahogany and glass counter handing medicine to customers. Behind them on the dark wooden shelves were large white porcelain containers; displayed on them in gold cursive writing were the names of drugs like *Belladonna* and *Folium Digitalis*.

Then she would have called her brothers. Uncle Anker was my mother's older brother by two years. Their younger brother, Kristian, lived in Copenhagen.

Meanwhile we kids walked around the house on tiptoes.

Evenings, we usually sat around the dining room table doing our homework while my mother darned socks or knitted. Bedstefar might listen to the radio. Thursdays there was our favorite show, *Familien Hansen*. While Bedstefar was ill it seemed less enjoyable; we missed his caustic comments.

Bedstefar became delirious. Dr. Aggebo would have been concerned when the fever didn't break and my mother then must have realized her father was dying.

Bedstefar's faith was of concern to my mother now that her father would soon be meeting his Maker. Her father had always been a bit of a rogue. He grew up the son of a farm laborer, one of eight siblings and half-siblings. He had been forced to work from age seven, and had left school at fourteen after seven years of a hit-and-miss education. His father had been abusive and had garnered his wages until he was eighteen. My own father thought this might have accounted for Bedstefar sometimes seeming to have a chip on his shoulder. He worked on farms until he married in 1892 at age twenty-eight. He then found a more stable job working on the railroads. His bride,

Alfrida, was Swedish. She had left her home on the island of Inlängan off the coast of Karlskrona at age sixteen after her family could no longer support her. She had worked as a maid on a large farm. Her home had been more stable, though equally poor, but she had had a Christian upbringing, which Bedstefar had not. Bedstefar was tough, and it must have been difficult at times for the more placid Alfrida. She wanted him to go to church with her, but he was determined to foil her attempts to get him there. Week after week, she went to church alone, week after week he stayed at home on Sunday mornings.

Then in 1905, there was a religious revival in the area where they lived. About a week before the revival meetings began, Bedstemor Alfrida was struck dumb. She couldn't speak a word. She had to write everything she wanted to say on a board. The doctor did not know the reason for this and could give no hope she would recover. Bedstefar might have wondered if this was God speaking to him, but Bedstemor knew this was the work of the Lord. Within eight days, Bedstefar became a believer, and their joy was great. Within another week, Bedstemor was able to speak again. She knew that God had cured her. My mother had some memory of this. She was nine years old at the time and had been frightened by her mother's inability to speak. She was convinced that God had had a role in the events.

Since then Bedstefar had faithfully attended church with Bedstemor and had never again mocked her faith, yet my mother might have worried that his heart wasn't in it. He often lapsed into cussing.

Then one evening the minister came, as did uncle Anker, aunt Jenny and Dr. Aggebo. Bedstefar was now lost in a delirium. Singing and praying they stood around his bed. I was in bed next door as I heard them singing the darkest, saddest song I had ever heard: *Tunge, mørke natteskyer over himlen drage*, about the end of the day when dusk sets in, when loneliness and fear of the dark threaten you, when the heaviness of the silent night enfolds you. I was sure then that Bedstefar was dying.

The next morning, however, the fever broke and Bedstefar fell into a heavy sweat-drenched slumber. Later in the day we children snuck into his bedroom, frightened at what we might see, but there he was, sitting up in bed, his temperature down, his voice, yet weak from the fever, quavering with triumph and good-humored spite. Bedstefar was almost back to his own self.

"So you thought you were going to get rid of me. That hymn was sad enough to make a person wish he were dead. But I fooled you! Yes, I fooled you!"

When Dr. Aggebo came by a few days later to see him, Bedstefar was gone. He had decided it was time to get out of bed. My mother was startled to see him coming down the stairs in his dark woolen pants and jacket, his black railway worker's cap atop his white curly hair, his handlebar mustache all waxed again.

"I think I'll go for a walk in the woods. Spring is here and it's time I go check out those Spanish onions," he said and was gone.

"So the bird has flown the coop." Dr. Aggebo said.

Bedstefar lived another five years and died while my parents, Anna, and I were in Aden. I always remember him with great fondness.

A Lesson Learned

My friends and I had slung our skates over our shoulders and chased each other through the streets of our neighborhood to the woods. These woods framing the Bay of Aarhus had always been a refuge for our family. Here Bedstefar exercised his eighty-two-year old body; here we went to swim at the beach club, Den Permanente; here in spring the Spanish onions first made their appearance, then the anemones that we picked and brought home, and finally the beeches erupted into huge showers of pale green leaves that formed a canopy far above the forest floor. Now it was winter, however, and the trees were bare, snow covered the ground, and we were on our way to the pond in the middle of the forest.

We screwed on our skates with the rusty skating keys we carried on strings around our necks, screwing them tight onto the soles of our well-worn boots, and fastened the straps. My skates were rusty as well as dull. With my father gone, there was no one to sharpen them. The ice was perfect and there were many people out on this Sunday afternoon.

We had likely been in church that morning. Surprisingly, despite my family's regular church attendance I have no recollection of being in church during my childhood years in Aarhus. Yet my brother-in-law's parents, parishioners of Sct. Johannes Kirke (St. John's Church) would relate how on Sundays they used to see the missionaries Borch-Jensen and their many children filing into church. That I do not remember being in church probably derives from the fact that pastors, dressed in black gowns with white ruffs, preached overly theological sermons from the pulpit, in unctuous voices that should have put a child to sleep. No doubt the peal of the organ must have fascinated me as it swelled and rose to the vaults of the church where the notes seemed to play tag with each other. I also loved to sing, and to this day I know a multitude of Danish hymns by heart.

After church we had likely gone to Sunday school at the Mission House. I have positive memories of this place where we often had fun chasing each other down the long hallways. But I also remember being quiet in Sunday school and listening to Bible Stories and singing. In particular I remember learning to sing "Thy little ones, dear Lord, are we." I also remember being enraptured with the ceilings where angels rested on puff clouds, smiling at each other and at the children below. I wondered if that was how it would be in heaven and when I died, would I be sitting on a pink cloud looking down on the earth?

We were often at the Mission House; if not for Sunday School, then for meetings and bazaars. I liked the bazaars where I enjoyed eating *lagkage* (layered cake). The lagkage with its three or four layers of cake separated by jam or cream, the whole thing topped with whipping cream was appetizing beyond words. Layered cake always later reminded me of the Mission House.

My mother often hosted a booth there on Mission Days with exhibits of pictures and artifacts from Aden. She talked with passion about the mission, telling people about the Arab children and about the women in Aden, and that though some wanted to become Christians the men in their families prohibited it. When there were no visitors to her booth, my mother sat chatting with the other women; my mother loved to talk and share gossip.

At the skating pond my friends and I chased each other, dashing in and out between sedately skating older couples, sometimes sliding right into them. But the weather was becoming gloomy and damp, tufts of fog sneaked in between the treetops. After exhausting ourselves completely we decided to set off for home. We made our way through the woods along a road that brought us to Grenåvej, a durable concrete exit road out of the city the Germans had built.

Suddenly I realized I needed to pee and ran toward the entrance of a bunker. Dried grass and snow covered it, submerged as it was in the ground. The bunkers had been part of life during the war, but now no one used them. Yet, the bunker offered privacy when one was in my predicament.

I rushed down the stairs—I felt like holding my nose, the place had an undeniable odor—but quickly I slipped inside and ran to squat in a corner. I had just finished when I heard someone behind me. I froze and quickly pulled up my pants.

"No, no, leave your pants down." I was startled by the man's voice. I expected no one to be there. In fact, I had seen no one, but of course, it was dark, little light came through the small hole that served as a window. Scared, I turned around.

"You should not be peeing here. Pull your pants down so I can smack your bottom. You have been a naughty girl," the man said.

His words seemed preposterous, spoken as they were by someone who was a complete stranger to me. I don't know if I could have articulated then what I felt, but I knew something was very wrong. I would later be able to use language for the man's behavior. Maybe I should not have been peeing there, but the man did not have the authority to punish me, only my parents did. Besides, he seemed like a person who had no authority at all.

I began moving toward the exit, but he stood in my way and grabbed my arm. In anger I started screaming at him.

"You let me go! Get out of my way!" I wrested my arm from his hand and pounced on him. My fists hammered away at his chest. "You let me go, let me out of here!"

My sudden fury must have caught him off guard, and I was able to slip by him. I ran out of the bunker as fast as I could.

I was eleven years old then, and I knew the man had bad intentions, yet I don't remember being terribly frightened. More than anything I was angry, but my anger was nothing compared to my mother's. She was shaken and she let me know that I had a right to be angry; in fact this fit very well with her view of men.

"You have to be careful of men," were words often spoken. "They only have one thing on their mind."

Diverging Paths

My mother was overwhelmed. There was so much to take care of. Fortunately my father was there to help. The rest of us had our assigned jobs. It was close to Christmas 1949, we were packing up, preparing to leave for Aden, and the house was in turmoil. There were advantages to being poor; we had few material goods to dispose of.

My father had come back toward the end of 1948, ending the latest of my parents' many separations. On my father's return Bedstefar went into a nursing home; he could not live with us once Marius was home, he said; both were stubborn and it would have led to clashes. Fortunately, it turned out that Bedstefar loved the nursing home. Many of his old cronies were there, and he loved the nurses. Frida said Bedstefar was trying to get fresh with them, goosing them. I am sure that was not what my mother hoped to hear, but knowing her father, she realized it was within the realm of possibility. We children often stopped to see him, especially Frida, his favorite; she was then a journalist apprentice, and Bedstefar frequently rewarded her with much needed extra pocket money.

Now the three of us, my mother, Anna Margrethe who was nine, and I twelve were preparing to return to Aden with my father. We had spent six years in the house on Hans Egedesvej; here we had been together as a family except for the two years my father had been in Aden. Here we had grown up and now the oldest of my siblings were on their way out into the world. My parents had made sure they had good schooling and now it was up to them to make the best of it. Frida had quit her journalism apprenticeship and had taken off for England where she had citizenship because of her birth in Aden. She wanted to try her wings.

My mother usually started preparations for Christmas in the beginning of December, baking all the cookies we loved, *brunekager, vanillekranse, pebernødder, jødekager*, and making red and white marzipan candy. She sealed the boxes and hid them so we wouldn't raid them before Christmas, yet we always managed to filch some. But that year she baked little, just enough to get us through Christmas.

When we finally sat down for Christmas dinner on the twenty-fourth my mother was exhausted. Bedstefar was there for the evening. The table was set with the best china, the Wedgwood Hague pattern of Dutch windmills my mother inherited from her mother. Tantalizing, the roast goose stood in the middle of the table. Small red-and-white Danish paper flags waved from its top. None of us could wait to put our teeth into its succulent meat, eating it with *rødkål*, lingonberries, caramelized potatoes, and gravy as accompaniment. Everyone around the table was filled with anticipation, not just for the sumptuous dinner, not for the gifts, which really did not usually generate great expectations, but for what lay ahead of each of us.

Our home as we had known it until then, would dissolve and the family disperse. Johs, my only brother, was soon to be nineteen. He had grown into a handsome young man, tall and slim, his dark blond hair already thinning slightly at the temples, taking after my father. He was quiet and shy, quiescent almost. He had gone off to boarding school at fifteen and during the last year he had worked on a farm, for a farmer of my parents' acquaintance, as he had had no clue what he wanted to do with his life. But with some prodding, he had decided he would like to become a teacher and he was to start a prep class before gaining entrance.

My father smiled at my mother from the other end of the table. He was serene. As usual, he took transitions in stride and he would be happy going back to Aden with my mother at his side. Bedstefar was gnawing away at a bone; he didn't want to leave one scrap of meat. It would be hard for all of us to say good-bye to Bedstefar. We might not see him again. Though Bedstefar had no complaints, it was clear that at eighty-five anything could happen to him.

My father started clearing the plates. Mother brought in a heaping bowl of *risengrød* (rice porridge), a carafe of warm mead, cinnamon-sugar, and butter. Everyone helped themselves to a serving, making a depression in the middle of the porridge for butter, sprinkling it with cinnamon-sugar, and pouring on the warm mead.

"I just love this, Mum," I said, "why don't we have this everyday?"

"We only have this at Christmas," my mother said in a definitive and preoccupied voice.

My sister Elin was sixteen then. I don't think anyone worried much about her. She was resourceful, practical, with both feet firmly planted on the ground. She knew her own mind, and my mother and she had had many arguments. But Elin could also look sweet and angelic at times; with her dimples and high cheekbones she could display a beatific smile, though when her snubbed nose and her questioning eyes flared she was like an imperious Furie, I sometimes thought. She would live in the home of a pastor friend of my parents.

"Do you think I'll get the almond this year?" Anna asked as she gingerly tapped into her rice porridge with a spoon looking for the almond. Finding the hidden almond was always the big excitement of our Danish Christmas meal. Whoever found it, received a prize. But had Johs or Elin found it and weren't telling? If so, maybe she should help herself to more, Anna would have thought. Maybe the almond was still in the bowl.

"Finish what you have on your plate, before you take more," Mum said.

I no longer remember who got the almond and what the prize was at that Christmas dinner in 1949. Did we have marzipan pigs like my family does now?

After dinner my father went to light the Christmas tree in the living room and when done he threw open the doors to its glory. He had decorated it the night before, and no one had seen it until this moment. That was part of the magic of Christmas, the tree that no one saw until it was revealed to us in all its magnificence. When we were little, we were always in awe of it. My father read the Christmas gospel and offered his prayers of thanksgiving to God who so bountifully cared for us. Then we got up to "dance" around the

Christmas tree, singing the old well-known Danish Christmas hymns.

We shared gifts. There weren't many and they were mostly utilitarian, things we needed anyway. We plundered the Christmas tree, stripped it of all the little goodies hidden in the colorful homemade glossy paper baskets and played guessing games with the peppernuts.

The New Year would auger in a new life for all of us. My parents, Anna, and I would leave Denmark on December 29, 1949 closing the chapter on my Danish childhood.

The author's great-great-grandparents, Frederik and Johanne Borch.

The author's father's family, 1902. Back row from left: Andreas, Viggo, Erhard;
front row from left: Inger, Erhardine (Dine) Borch-Jensen, and the author's father, Marius.

The author's mother, 1924.

The author's father in Aden, 1938.

The author's parent's wedding at the British Legation in Addis Abeba, Ethiopia, 1927.

The author's siblings and mother: sister Frida, mother,
the author, sister Elin, and brother Johs in Denmark, 1938

The author's sisters Elin and Frida and brother Johs, with the author in pram, Aarhus, 1939.

The author's sister Anna with her father and mother and the author in Aden 1953.

Bedstemor and Bedstefar (the author's maternal grandparents) Mikkel Peter Christensen and Alfrida Mathilde (Göransson) Christensen in the 1920s (above) and 1940 (below).

Aden

(1949–1953)

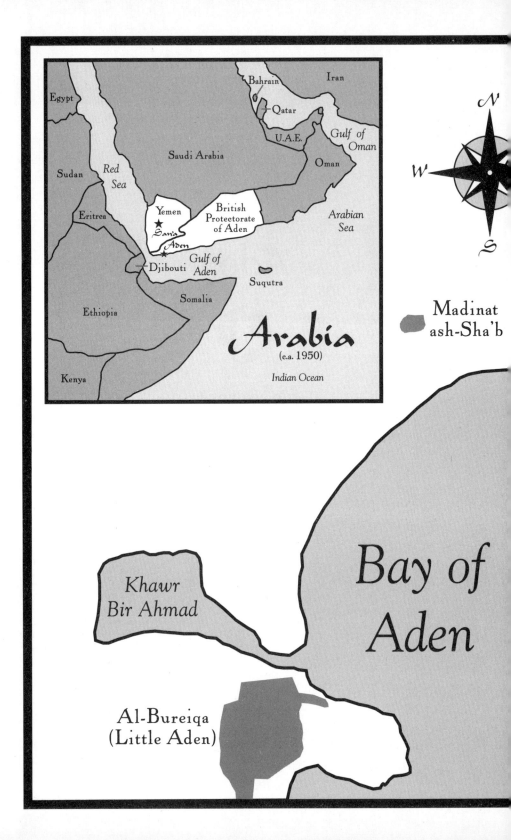

Bahrain

Iran

Qatar

U.A.E.

Gulf of
Oman

Egypt

Saudi Arabia

Oman

Sudan

Red
Sea

Arabian
Sea

Eritrea

Yemen

British
Protectorate
of Aden

★ San'a
Aden ★

Gulf of
Aden

Djibouti

Suqutra

Somalia

Ethiopia

Arabia
(c.a. 1950)

Kenya

Indian Ocean

N

W

S

Madinat
ash-Sha'b

Bay of
Aden

Khawr
Bir Ahmad

Al-Bureiqa
(Little Aden)

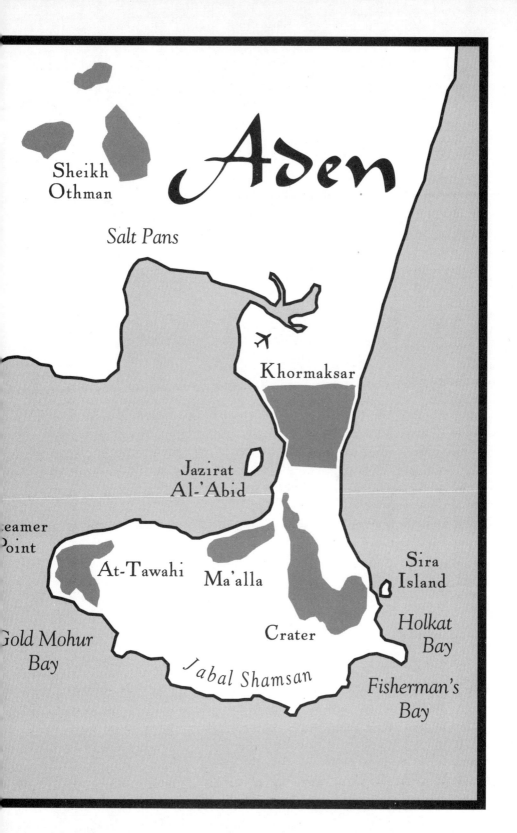

Wonder…

Aden is the pleasantest and most beautiful city in all of Arabia.
It is enclosed by great walls on the side of the sea and by mountains
on the side of the land. On top of these mountains several castles are
clearly visible…it lies beyond the Red Sea, at the edge of the great ocean.
— SAMSON, 1683

Standing on deck as the ship put down anchor at Steamer Point, I keenly followed everything in the harbor—the freighters, the passenger ships, and the launches going back and forth. The dhows were alluring with their pointed bows, oblique sterns, and peculiar, billowing jib sails; it felt like stepping into a tale from Arabian Nights. Sindhbad the Sailor set out on his merchant expeditions in ships like these.

I wished I could go ashore immediately. Impatiently I watched as the customs boat pulled alongside the ship. Then came the Health Officer in his launch and with him Dr. Walker, the missionary physician who was meeting us and taking us to shore. Then, after the adults had talked endlessly, after the Customs Officer had cleared all the papers, and after the Health Officer had approved our health certificates, we were finally ready to leave the ship and go ashore.

I had not at all minded leaving Aarhus to come here. I had heard about Aden all my life; my parents and older siblings had lived so long in this fabled place; Anna and I alone had never been privileged to visit here. I had enthusiastically embraced the idea of going to Aden, caring little that I left friends behind; I could probably get along without them for a while. Besides, I would be making lots of new friends, I was sure.

We had left right after Christmas. Johs and Elin had been at the Main Railway Station in Aarhus to say goodbye. That Elin could be so calm knowing her parents, Anna and I would move so far away, baffled me. At sixteen Elin hadn't minded that she had a home no more. Her move to live with friends of our parents until graduating from the Gymnasium appeared to exhilarate her; with exuberance she looked forward to the freedom that awaited her, escaping at last from what she considered an oppressive childhood.

All of Elin exuded confidence, I thought: her five foot four inch slender frame, her blond permed hair, and her broad smile, a smile that pushed her prominent cheekbones higher and crinkled her eyes. How could she be so happy? I thought ruefully. How could she care so little that we were leaving? But just then, tears filled the corners of Elin's eyes. Oh, wonder of all wonders, she did mind after all. As my sister's brow furrowed and her eyes grew bigger and brighter, I felt reassured. Yes, she *did* care. Elin's usually impish and playful smile was now questioning and wistful. Was she on the verge of bursting into tears? Normally she was lively and outgoing, occasionally temperamental—indeed, her mood swings could be significant—when she was happy she was so radiant and energetic and her eyes shone with amusement; but now they were filled with sadness.

Johs, nineteen however, had looked diffident. Amiable though he was, I didn't know him well as he had been gone for two or three years. Though he had not attended the Gymnasium, he had been accepted into the prep class at the local Teachers' College where he planned to get a teaching degree. He had moved in with Pastor Bøss, other friends of our parents.

There had been a hustle and bustle at the train station, people getting on and off trains, running across platforms, and up and down stairs to catch their connections, busy holiday travelers returning home after spending Christmas with family. My mother gave last minute instructions to Johs and Elin. Then my father, his voice breaking with emotion, admonished them one last time.

I felt torn apart by the leave-taking. As leaves from a damaged book, my feelings were flung across the platform, the pages blown around by the wind, caught and lifted up, twirled around on eddies of air. Would I ever be able to gather them and put them back together again?

Finally, the train pulled away from the platform.

"Take good care of yourselves, and write…write long letters…," Elin's voice trailed away as the train moved out of the station and picked up speed. As it rounded a curve, she and Johs suddenly disappeared from our view.

During the subsequent train journey, we were all subdued. Outside the landscape languished in a steady drizzle, desolate and gray. White and black cows, their hooves buried in the wet pasture, cast indolent glances after the train. Unable to take my eyes off the countryside, I savored it all; I would be away from Denmark for a long time. I curled up in a corner, clasping my shoulders. Outside everything was bleak, yet the fields held such promise, and soon the pastures would be green again. This matched my feelings: sadness at leaving, yet anticipation and excitement about the future; from now on nothing would be familiar or predictable anymore.

In Antwerp we stayed at the Seamen's Mission while my father made sure our boxes were loaded onto the SS *Mahenge*, the freighter we would be traveling on. Frida came to Antwerp from England to say goodbye to us and Anna and I were excited to see her again. I have a black-and-white picture of her sitting outside a hotel in Antwerp. She was almost twenty-one years old then; a tiny young woman, compact in a bulky winter coat, with hands folded in her lap; her legs with feet in sensible flat shoes are crossed at the ankles. The light illumes one side of her face and hair as though only part of her is visible and available; she doesn't smile. Her face is raised in detachment.

I loved the voyage to Aden, a whole two weeks onboard a ship. There were few passengers and the crew onboard the freighter were friendly, especially the first mate who let Anna and me tag along as he went about his duties. During our dinners, we sat at the captain's table, a table covered with a beautiful white damask tablecloth, matching napkins, wine glasses, and flowers in a vase.

On its way across the Bay of Biscay the ship pitched through the seas with waves towering over it. Anna and I walked the decks with wide-based gaits laughing with excitement as the spray drenched us. In the dining room, the crew raised the rims of the tables and wet down the tablecloths to prevent plates, glasses, and silverware from sliding off. While our father, Anna, and I continued to enjoy our meals, our mother retreated to the cabin below, defeated by seasickness.

We sailed past the Rock of Gibraltar and scanned the rocks for the Barbary Apes our father told us lived there, but we saw none. We docked first in Genoa and then in Livorno where we visited the Leaning Tower of Pisa. And finally, we sailed through the Straits of Messina where Mt. Etna spewed lava into the sky like fireworks on New Year's Eve. What a farewell Europe was giving us.

I had looked forward to setting foot in Egypt. My father's stories about *al-misr* (Egypt) had created images in my mind of undulating desert sands stretching to the horizon, of camels and donkeys, and of Egyptians in red fezes and long shirt-like gowns, and above all of sun and heat. Therefore I was much surprised at how gray and rainy it was as we approached Egypt; the sea was black and impenetrable. I stood in the bow of the ship, staring towards the horizon over which I expected Egypt to appear, but in the gray haze, sky and sea came together. Eventually the hazy line I decided must be the horizon gradually thickened and Egypt emerged from the sea. Hours later, we were at anchor in Port Said. Now the clouds dispersed and it became hot.

We spent the day ashore where smells of camels, goats, coffee, incense, and sand assaulted our senses; the people shouted, argued, and laughed in that strange, guttural language, Arabic. Would I ever learn it?

Then we continued on, passed through the Suez Canal, all the way down the Red Sea, through the Bab el Mandeb Strait, and finally, an early morning, the bare volcanic rocks of Aden appeared on the horizon as little dots. They grew until they were like pyramids in a mirage, surrounded by shimmering sea, and within hours the ship passed by the looming extinct volcano into the Bay of Aden.

I said hello to Dr. Walker. His welcome was warm. Gawky and cheery, his cheeks ruddy, his dark hair bristly, he spoke in a rolling Scottish accent. He wore a khaki topee, long, khaki *ghurka* shorts, and knee-high socks, just like my father.

Then we were ashore. Barefoot beggar children swarmed around us, shouting "Baksheesh!" They were so persistent that I wished I could give them something so they would leave, but my father, cold-hearted, it seemed, shooed them away and I, despite the boys' near nakedness—they wore only a short, dirty loincloth—failed to realize that they were utterly impoverished, that they were street children, orphans doomed to care for themselves because of the harsh reality of their family's poverty.

"Hop in, and off we'll be. Karen and the kiddies are waiting," Dr. Walker said. Like all Land Rovers in Aden, Dr. Walker's was dusty, inside and out. My bare legs quickly became covered with patches of grayish-brown dirt and my dress clung to the seat. Yet, I was excited; it was too much to grasp that we would actually be living here, at first with Dr. Walker and his family at Kintore. I wondered what their house was like. I looked forward to meeting his children and hoped I could understand them.

Looking across the Bay of Aden, I tried to imagine where their house might be. It was not in Crater, I knew, which was in the volcano behind us, but in the desert near Sheikh Othman.

"About ten miles in that direction…," Dr. Walker pointed. All I saw was sand; the horizon was gray and indistinct. Then I glimpsed a tower and some airplanes on the other side of the Bay. "…no, that's the RAF Airport at Khormaksar," Doctor Walker laughed. " We're a little north of that, in the desert. You can't see our house from here."

The Land Rover later became a symbol for me of my years in Aden. I fell in love with it; it brought me so many adventures. However, on the threshold of this my new life, my fascination was with riding in a car, in any car—I could not remember ever riding in one—and particularly in a jeep. From the backseat I looked out across the hood and realized there was no windshield, it had been folded down; neither were there windows in the doors.

"That's to keep you cool as you drive," Dr. Walker said with a grin. I understood most of what he said.

My mother sat with us two girls in the back. She seemed happy, but also tired and hot. I was not always sure how my mother felt. She had so looked forward to being back, but now that we were here she somehow seemed a little apprehensive. She pursed her lips and massaged the stump of the right middle finger, the finger she lost to infection some years ago. I knew this was a sure sign of anxiety.

My mother, however, seldom lost for words, soon rose to the occasion, and told us about everything we saw along our way. We passed the Crescent—the shopping area—a half-moon-shaped row of buildings containing larger shops fronted by a small garden.

"Oh, nothing has changed," my mother marveled.

"And this is where we'll shop for material for clothes." She pointed to a large store where bolts and bolts of brightly colored cloth stood on end in such dense clusters that shoppers could barely make their way through the store.

Everything was so bright and cheery.

In the midst of the garden, a statue of the seated Queen Victoria overflowed its marble support. How strange and incongruous her statue seemed in these surroundings. Arab men clothed in bright futas (loin cloths), shirts, and colorful crocheted hats sat on their haunches around the foot of the statue, talking, gesticulating, eating sambusas (spicy and similar to eggrolls, but triangular), all the while paying not the least attention to this the motherly former Ruler of the Mighty British Empire.

Dr. Walker wanted to give Anna and me a taste of the market, the souq. The crowds were immense. I became aware of the many nationalities and my mother discreetly pointed them out: Arabs, Indians, Somalis, Jews, and of course the occasional European. Animals mingled freely—goats, dogs, chickens, and donkeys. And there again were the enchanting smells—of incense, coffee, spices, sun, sand, and of many things with which I was as yet unfamiliar, pungent not at all unpleasant smells. From small stores, mere holes in the wall, merchants hawked utensils, food staples, cloth, watches, and jewelry, anything one might wish for. I stared in amazement. I thought of the shopping street at home in Aarhus, how drab it was in comparison to this. Now, in January, the downtown streets of Aarhus were wet and dank; rain and fog must have settled in, daylight hours were few, and the sun was absent for days on end, covered by dark, heavy clouds. I felt stimulated, alive, and excited here where color, sun, and warmth surrounded me.

We continued our slow progress through the souq. In rooms giving onto the street old men sat on rope grid beds, smoking pipes made of elaborately designed brass; in other rooms younger men reclined against the walls, languidly talking and chewing away.

"That's qat they are chewing, mildly narcotic green leaves that makes them forget everything. They sit and chew it all day and get nothing done."

My mother's condemnation caused me no surprise. My mother tended toward open display of her disapproval. I realized there were very few women in the market. The ones I saw were all dressed in black from head to toe—in chadors—their eyes hidden behind a gauze-like colored veil. What is it like walking around inside that black tent? I wondered.

We drove through Ma'alla and north, away from the volcano. We passed by the RAF camp, which was strongly protected by barbed wire fencing and guards. Within its perimeter were the many barracks for the men and some single-family houses for the officers. The British had a significant force stationed here.

Beyond the camp, white fields stretched all the way west to the Bay: saltpans, my mother explained.

The sky was blue without a cloud and the day was getting warmer. In front of us stretched the desert; a haze hovered over everything. I was now convinced that I could never miss Denmark. This place excited me. I couldn't wait to explore my new environment; I couldn't wait to learn English; neither could I wait to learn Arabic so I could get to know the people who lived here.

Then we saw the large pale-yellow house. It seemed to lie there all by itself in the middle of the desert, surrounded by tall mud walls. We swung through the gates, up to the main entrance. The house was rectangular; a porch surrounded it on the bottom floor, large pillars supported the veranda above. Occasional bushes of oleander grew against the pillars; scattered palm trees and thorny acacias dotted the compound.

We had arrived at our destination.

Confronting the Past

*Aden is a crossroads of several sea routes staked out by lighthouses
and little islands bristling with cannon; it is one of the links in the long
chain that maintains the profits of London businessmen around the world.
A port of call full of murderous symbols, a companion piece to Gibraltar.*
— PAUL NIZAN, 1926

I can only imagine what it must have meant to my parents, and especially my mother to be back in Aden. It was twelve years since she had left with four-year-old Elin and with me in her belly. During that time our family had grown to seven members; we had lived through a World War and German occupation; and my parents had experienced four years of separation. They were now fifty-four and fifty-three. They were back to pursue work to which they had dedicated their lives. Though it wasn't backbreaking work, one could easily feel defeated by it. Their mission to convert Muslims to Christianity was difficult, if not impossible. Only their great faith sustained them.

The day we first arrived I had seen my mother looking at the bare rocks of Aden. Rocks and sand was all it was. Yet to her, it was a beautiful and welcoming sight. The rocks were immutable and unchanging. For thousands of years the hot volcanic rocks surrounding Crater had remained the same. They were so barren it was amazing that anything could grow on them. But scattered trees and bushes grew in crevices of the frozen lava, seemingly taking their moisture and nourishment from the air. My parents in their work must at times have felt as parched as the rocks and must have felt that God had forgotten them, that there was no answer to their prayers that the vineyards be fruitful. Sometimes it must have been terribly discouraging for them that Christ's message was not taking hold in the Muslim world. Yet they might have thought that those trees, tapping into a water source so deep within the mountain, were a wonderful illustration to them of how they also could continue to tap into the water source they knew was God's promise to them.

My parents were surely also looking forward to seeing some of their Christian Arab friends again, one of them Mubarak Ibrahim, their first Christian. He was a stalwart presence at the Danish Mission Book Store, of which he had been in charge since his conversion in 1922. Mubarak was an audacious yet timid man: audacious because he had bravely embraced Christianity, timid because he dared not witness about Christ to his fellow Muslims.

Mubarak had come to Aden as a young child, an orphan, his entire family and tribe having been eradicated by smallpox. When he was about ten years old he had heard a Christian preach and had been so taken with the word of the Christian God that when he encountered the Gospel again at age sixteen he immediately decided to become a Christian. He was baptized and had been a staunch follower of Christ since then. Nonetheless, the missionaries had never been able to persuade him to evangelize. People might kill him for witnessing to Christ. Although outright murder was unlikely under British rule, there were other ways of making a man disappear and this knowledge was a powerful deterrent for Mubarak.

Yet at times he surprised my parents. Once he gave his Bible away to someone who, when seeing Mubarak read it, had expressed a desire to read it too. On another occasion, though reluctant to be seen with the missionaries, he accompanied one of them on an evangelizing trip to his home province, and to the missionary's great surprise Mubarak admitted to being a Christian and exposed himself to threats, anger, and hostility from his people.

He must have been a lonely man. He had few friends; he never married and had no extended family, yet he did not seek any closeness with the missionaries. He insisted on remaining an Arab, always maintaining his Arab dress. Yet he had always been steadfast and had never reverted to Islam. Others who were baptized had obviously mainly sought worldly gain and status among the Europeans, but when times became tough, they deserted

Christianity. Not so Mubarak, who had now been a Christian for twenty-eight years.

When my mother had first heard that we would be living with the Walkers, she must have been unhappy. Mrs. Walker was the Danish nurse with whom my father had traveled to San'a in 1938, with whom he had shared a tent on the way, and for whom (presumably unbeknownst to her) he had felt such a powerful attraction. She had since married Dr. Walker. My mother must have wondered how it would be to live in the same house as Karen Walker? And though my father would have assured her that it would be fine, my mother may have feared a resurgence of her jealousy.

At Kintore my parents stepped out of the Land Rover to greet Mrs. Walker, a tall, statuesque, blond woman. She welcomed them warmly in Danish and introduced us to her towheaded children, the oldest of whom was about eight. My parents returned Mrs. Walker's greeting, my father with his usual quiet, apologetic laughter. My mother launched into nervous, urgent speech.

"Let me show you your room," Karen said as they moved up the stairs to the second floor.

"Oh, this is the room where I gave birth to Frida," I heard my mother exclaiming.

The birth of my sister Frida was connected to another devastating memory for my mother. I learned of this when I read my parents' memoirs. Another missionary woman had—it seemed—almost staked a claim to my father even before he and my mother met. Meta was her name. My father had trained with her in England and they had spent some time together in Cairo, but my father claimed he was never attracted to her and that he never encouraged her. He thought of Meta as a colleague and friend, and treated her as such. If only Meta had accepted that she meant nothing to my father, things would have been fine. But she hadn't, and my father wasn't always sensitive to how this affected my mother. Sometimes he could be unintentionally selfish.

Meta had hurt my mother deeply before my parents' wedding—something my mother did not tell my father until several years later—by saying to her that she, Meta, should have been the one to marry my father. Then later, while my mother was pregnant with Frida, Meta one day had asked my father to go hiking with her, well knowing my mother couldn't go. My father had wanted to; he loved hiking. This became cause for an argument between my parents, neither of whom could see the other's point of view. But my father had not gone on the hike. To my mother it must often have seemed that my father was cruelly insensitive.

Yet the worst came after Frida was born. Though my parents lived and worked in Crater, the delivery took place at Kintore in Sheikh Othman where the obstetrician lived. Miss Andersen, the older missionary nurse, had promised to attend the delivery, but the day my mother went into labor she had been unable to come and had instead sent Meta, who was not a nurse. My parents felt they could not refuse her, but both were upset. The delivery went well and my father returned to Crater the next day to teach at the Danish Mission's Boys' School. When he came back to Kintore in the evening, Meta met him at the door, told him my mother was asleep and meanwhile, would he like to take a walk with her, Meta? My father had been inside all day, and needed the fresh air, so he agreed. My mother, however, had not been asleep. Anxious to see my father, she had gotten up when she heard his car, and as she looked out the French doors of the very room she was now to occupy, she had seen him walk away with Meta. She could not understand this. Here she was with their first-born, waiting for him. I am not sure my father ever understood how hurtful this was to my mother.

Nonetheless—my parents now were back in Sheikh Othman and working at the Scottish Mission because the Danish Mission in Crater had no available housing at the time and the Scottish Mission needed an evangelist. We were to stay there about a year-and-a-half before moving to Crater.

...And More Wonder

I jumped out of my seat in the Land Rover. So this is it, this is Kintore, I thought, looking up at the house. Trelliswork surrounded the front part of the porch downstairs. A veranda surrounded the upstairs level as well. Mrs. Walker introduced us to her children.

"Hello," Dorothy said, "and welcome. We have looked forward to meeting you." That was quite a mouthful for a child who looked to be about eight. Dorothy was the oldest and I would soon find that she was the self appointed ruler of the roost, motherly and directive towards her younger siblings, and at times insufferably mature for her age. David was a rambunctious boy of five and Elspeth a lovely wisp of a three-year-old. They were immensely excited by this influx of new children and the fact that Anna and I only spoke and understood little English was quickly forgotten as we all ran off to explore the outside.

The Walker children first took us to meet the monkey who lived in one of the acacia trees. The monkey was chained to the tree.

"Why the chain?" I asked.

"Well, at first he wasn't chained," Dorothy said, "but he was all over the house, getting into everything, so we had to make sure he stayed in one place. Also, he is not very gentle. He bites and pinches whenever he gets a chance. So we really don't like him very much." I wasn't sure I understood everything, but gathered the monkey was not a favorite pet.

I took in the garden. There was no grass, just sand; one giant sandbox. Palm trees were scattered here and there, surrounded by troughs that connected to similar troughs around bushes bearing vividly purple flowers; this was clearly some kind of watering system. It really wasn't much of a garden I thought, certainly not what we'd call a garden back home.

We went to the back entry to the compound. Dorothy opened it.

"We are not really supposed to go outside." Dorothy said, " and at night this door is always locked, so strangers can't get in."

"So robbers can't get in!" David said.

We played in the compound; I entertained Elspeth by giving her piggy-back rides. Finally, at the end of the afternoon, we went to one of the mud houses at the bottom of the garden. Through an open door, Dorothy talked in Arabic to someone inside the house who invited us in. Jealously I noted how easily Dorothy switched from one language to the other. A young Arab woman stood bent over a bed. She turned around and smiled. A scarf cov-ered her oiled, glistening black hair. A brightly colored short-sleeved dress fell to her henna colored bare feet. Gracefully she lifted a beautiful baby off the bed, a baby girl with black curls, wearing a tiny dress without sleeves.

I stood at the threshold, looking at the woman, observing the room.

"As-salaam 'aleikum," the woman said.

"Wa 'aleikum as-salaam," I answered in the only Arabic I knew. My fa-ther had taught me this much.

The woman was Aïsha, the wife of Mustafa, the cook. I had never seen such simplicity and poverty before. The dark room had a dirt floor and brown mud walls; wood beams and branches supported the flat roof; the shutters of the window opening were closed. There were two rope grid beds along the walls covered with embroidered white sheets. I came to the slow realization that the entire family lived in this one room where there seemed to be nei-ther kitchen nor bathroom. Two little boys with runny noses came in from the outside clad only in short, dirty white shirts. The older, about three, helped the one year old across the step. I reached my hand out to the older. He grinned; saying nothing, he clutched my hand and I was immediately touched by his trust. Yet I hardly had time to take in any more before a gong sounded which called us back to the house for dinner. Reluctantly the boy let go of my hand.

The dining room had French doors toward the front and the back. The ceilings were high with a ceiling fan providing a gentle movement of air. The floor was smooth cement. My mother came down from the upstairs, happy, and rested after a nap. My father, restless after having missed exercise during the boat-trip, had taken a long walk with Bernard Walker from which he returned energized.

I found it jolly to be part of such a large family. I wasn't sure what I had expected, but this far exceeded anything I could have imagined. The table was set for the nine of us, and filled water glasses sweated onto the heavy, long table. Noisily we all scrambled into our seats and uncle Bernard—I had already been asked to call him that—said a long prayer in English thanking God for our safe arrival, asking Him to bless my father's work here and the meal of which we were about to partake. At least, that was how I interpreted the grace.

Now Mustafa brought in the food.

"Oh, we are having an Arabic dinner. What a surprise." My mother was nostalgic. "I haven't tasted real Arabic food in years. This is *ruz wa sanuna*," she explained to us.

The rice was sticky and lumpy, the sauce reddish-brown with vegetables and greasy meat floating in it.

"Goat meat," Dorothy whispered. If I had any concerns about eating goat meat, they were quickly dispelled, because I found the sauce and meat very tasty, as well as very spicy. This sure was very different from the *frik-adeller*, gravy, and potatoes I was used to. I quickly asked for seconds. There was also mango chutney on the table that I found very exotic tasting.

For dessert we had a custard with a mix of tropical fruits, few of which I had ever tasted before. I felt stuffed as I washed everything down with glass after glass of water.

Upstairs in the living room we had devotions before the younger children went to bed. My father read a text and talked about it for a while—a long while it seemed, Elspeth's eyes were drooping—and we sang English hymns that even my parents seemed to know by heart. How did they know all this? My father closed with a prayer.

I felt tired and sleepy as well. This had been a long and wondrous day. I didn't want it to end.

Feeling My Way

We had arrived in winter when nights in the desert were cool and that first night in our makeshift bedroom on the back veranda Anna and I curled up under several blankets. Crickets strummed their instruments; Arabic pop songs blared from loudspeakers in town; the sky was deep and dark, covered with a myriad of stars. Sleeping on the veranda was like sleeping outside; I could smell and hear the desert. I stretched out in bed, full of contentment and quickly fell asleep.

Crowing roosters woke us long before the sun peeked into our out-door bedroom. The repeated high-pitched, screechy braying of a donkey echoed between the houses in town. Mustafa's household came alive. I heard clanging of pots and pans from Aïsha's outdoor kitchen.

A soft shuffling, bare feet on wooden steps, now attracted my attention. I looked out through the trelliswork. It was the waterman. On his back, he carried a five-gallon can of water from the well. Up the outside backstairs he went, to the top of the house where he poured the contents of the cans into the reservoir that provided the house with running water. Up and down he went, and the splashing got softer as the tank filled.

"How does he do it?" I wondered, as I lay awake in my bed. "Wouldn't a pump be simpler?" In fact, I found that he was accorded no more attention than a pump. He was like the *gabarti*, the street sweepers and garbage men I later got to know, pariahs who stole around town like ghosts. He wore only a turban and the colorless futa I soon learned only the abysmally poor wore. He wasn't old, but his body was worn: his skin dry, scaly, the color of sand; his muscles stringy, no fat softening them; his feet bare. He barely hung on to life, I thought, yet he watered the desert garden, giving

life to the large shady palm trees and to the oleander and the bougainvil-
leas whose beauty left him indifferent; sustaining his family was his only
concern.

A pink light filled the veranda, and I got up, full of anticipation about
the new day. I looked out at the desert with its scattered, scraggly, thorny
bushes. Over everything floated a dome of deep blue cloudless sky. I felt I
was in a dream. The sun rose among the palm groves, bathing everything in
soft warm pastel hues. Part of me was still in Denmark, in the only reality I
had known so far, and I feared this new wondrous world might be nothing
but a mirage that would dissipate in a moment.

After breakfast, I met the laundress. She too had a shadowy existence,
I would realize. Tiny and skinny, barefoot, she sneaked up the backstairs
every midmorning. Once inside she took off her worn black chador revealing a faded dress unadorned by jewelry. She squatted over a basin in the
bathroom, washing the two families' clothes with a large, square bar of
brown soap, rinsing them in the bathtub, hanging them to dry on bushes
in the garden, then ironing them with a flatiron containing hot coals.

I tiptoed through the bathroom to get to the backstairs, smiling shyly at
the woman for whom I had no words yet, bashfully handing her dirty clothes
from the journey here. The washerwoman was a widow, with small children.
They sat quietly on the back-steps watching the white children play, too shy
to be induced to participate. I, tongue-tied, sat down beside them, watching
them intensely.

I didn't like that I couldn't talk to them, but then again, even if I could,
what would I say to them? I didn't know what was important to them, I had
no clue what their life was like. I must have patience and be happy that at
least I could communicate somewhat in English with the Walker family, I
thought. I found it easy to be around the younger children. Their sentences
were simple, and they seemed to ignore that Anna and I might not understand. Around them learning was easy.

Soon our days fell into a pattern. In the mornings my mother home schooled
us. In the afternoons we played with the Walker children. When after a
month the Walkers went on home leave, we played instead with the children of other missionaries. At times we went on picnics to the beach or to

the oasis gardens, and gradually Anna and I adjusted to our new surroundings and learned the basics of English.

An Ancient People

My mother loved this time of year in Aden. It was warm during the day and cool at night. She felt so unencumbered, she said, she wore only a thin cotton dress and was barefoot in light summer shoes.

My father started his work almost immediately: evangelizing work at the hospital, devotional and instructional meetings with the employees, and preaching in the hospital chapel on Sundays. There seemed to be enough to keep him busy.

My mother went with him to the hospital a couple of afternoons a week. No one could enter the women's wards as easily as she. It was no effort for her to engage these women in conversation. The ward was usually packed, not just the central ward, but also the large veranda encircling it. It was dark in there. Retractable mats, hanging at the periphery of the veranda, kept out not only stray looks, but also the sunlight. Women dressed in colorful dresses curled up on their rope grid beds, some not covered by blankets. Some were so sick they didn't even lift their heads when the *nasara* entered. My mother loved the term *nasara*. Arabs used it to refer to whites, but really, as my mother understood it, a *nasara* was a follower of the person from Nazareth, Jesus Christ, and my mother was proud to be known as such.

My mother seated herself on a chair in the middle of the room and soon women gathered around her, especially the healthy ones who were there to tend to family members. She read them Bible stories, from books with colored pictures. Soon it was quite crowded around her. All the women were full of curiosity; many of them were from the upcountry and some had never seen a white woman before. Yet, my mother didn't care why they listened to her, as long as she had the opportunity to tell them about her God and his son Jesus Christ. Afterwards she said a fervent prayer for their salvation.

In the evenings, we often sat on the second floor veranda, looking out across the desert enjoying the relative cool of the evening. The sun set in a flaming ball, lowering itself into the volcanic rocks of Al-Bureiqa, casting a blanket of gradually fading scarlet over the sands before it disappeared in the ocean beyond.

While sitting on the veranda, we saw below us, on the road beyond the mud-brick wall, a curious, continuous cortege of vehicles. Lorry after lorry filled with people passed Kintore and headed west on the gravel road toward Hiswa, the small village on the road to Al-Bureiqa. People stood, packed like sardines, in the back of the lorries; some even hung on to the outsides; they filled cars and taxis. Most were dusty and dirty. Some were beautifully dressed; many were in rags. They looked the way I had always imagined the people of the Bible looking. The men wore small black caps and had side-locks hanging to their shoulders; blue or black striped caftans covered their bodies like long nightshirts. Hoods, decorated with silver embroidery and beads, framed some of the women's faces. All were light-skinned and had fine, delicate facial features. Quietly they stood side by side hanging on to bundles of belongings. They often sang loudly and joyfully. Sometimes at night, I awakened to the hum of lorries and to the melancholy and haunt-ingly beautiful songs floating from them. My father told me these people were Jews from Yemen on their way to the Promised Land.

Apparently when my parents had lived in Aden in the twenties and thirties Jews had been a prominent feature of city life. They were well-es-tablished merchants who had lived there for many generations, yes, for cen-turies. By the 1950s most of these Aden Jews were gone, having emigrated to Israel.

The Yemeni Jews, however, were very unlike the city Jews. Watching them migrate left an indelible impact on me and many years later I learned their story. They had lived in exile and in great isolation in the interior of Yemen for two-and-a-half-thousand years and once had a Jewish kingdom there. In the capital city, San'a in Yemen, the Jews lived in their own quarter as merchants and silversmiths. Many other Yemeni Jews lived as farmers in small, remote villages. Through generations, they had passed on the promise from God of a return to Israel and somehow they had gotten word that there was a new Israel, that there was another "King David"—David Ben Gurion, the prime minister—and that Jews planned to rebuild the Temple. This must be the time to return, they believed. So the entire Jewish population of Yemen—60,000 in all –decided to pick up and leave. Many left their homes in the villages on foot. They had a long and difficult journey, across wild mountains, before they arrived in Aden. Fortunately, Jewish relief organizations had set up a camp at Hiswa, Camp Hashed, where they were cared for before traveling on to Israel. Dr. Bernard Walker—uncle Bernard—had been helping at the clinic in the camp. The Jewish relief organizations fed the survivors and made sure they got medical treatment, and when they were stronger, the organizations flew them to Israel. Every single night, planes left Aden. The planes were packed. Uncle Bernard had gone on one of them and told of how people were literally sitting in each other's laps. Many of them had never seen a plane before and were petrified when the plane rose into the sky. But they trusted in the fulfillment of a promise God had made to them that they should "mount up with wings as eagles." The relief organizations called this endeavor Operation Magic Carpet.

After five weeks, however my mother started feeling tired. She developed intermittent fevers, lost her appetite, had diarrhea, and noticed that the whites of her eyes were turning yellow. My parents sought the help of Dr. Alan Fawdry at the Government Hospital. After many tests, they learned she had amoebic dysentery. She had no energy; she barely made it out of bed during the day, and then only to rest in the living room. She lost weight. Even with treatment, she realized, it would be months before she was better. Our schooling became a concern, and after much consideration our parents finally made the decision to send us to the Catholic Girls' School in Steamer Point.

Catholic School

White billowing clothes, layers and layers of it covered her; only her face was visible. Not one strand of hair fell outside the wimple. She was very old. I took in every inch of her, all the way down to where feet in black stockings and black shoes appeared at the bottom of the flowing robes. I had never met a Roman Catholic nun before and was quietly amazed. The nun's bony hands appeared from under the long white sleeves as she extended them in greeting. They were pale, the skin almost translucent, blue veins coursed down their backs. I carefully put my hand in the nun's hand; it was cold and felt like tissue paper.

We were in the Reverend Mother's office at the Roman Catholic Girls' School in Steamer Point—the port city, fifteen kilometers away. The Reverend Mother's voice was gentle and warm, but frail. She spoke in an Irish brogue. She told us she had been here for forty-five years without interruption.

"That's a life time," my father said, politely and appropriately impressed by this commitment to the service of the Lord.

"Indeed," she said, "but Ireland is still in my heart and I will retire there soon. New nuns will be taking over."

My mother abruptly interrupted:

"We hope our girls won't be subjected to Catholic religious instruction."

The Reverend Mother smiled:

"No, they will not. We have girls of many religious persuasions here. Muslim, Hindu, Farsi, Greek Orthodox, and Indian Catholics from Portuguese Goa. We even have a Swedish Lutheran. Non-Catholics do not want their children influenced by our religion, so we restrict religious instruction to our Roman Catholic students."

My mother looked gratified by this statement. I was embarrassed. She didn't have to be so obviously pleased.

"But I do want to prepare you for the fact," the Reverend Mother said, "that many of our Muslim students leave school at age thirteen or fourteen, so Martha might soon find herself alone at her grade level."

Learning about Catholicism didn't matter to me, but being alone at my grade level was worrisome. I wanted to be with girls my own age.

I sat musing as I looked out the barred window to where students were at recess. All were dressed in identical white dresses with ties at the back. It seemed very strange to be going to an all-girls' school and to have to wear a uniform.

"That's the school yard for older students who need privacy," the Reverend Mother said and I realized that buildings without windows surrounded the small yard on the other sides; no one could look in. Teenaged Muslim girls could be there without chadors.

"We have a larger play ground out toward the street." Thank goodness, I thought.

At the end of the interview, I stepped out of the Mother Superior's office onto a veranda to explore the school. The veranda surrounded the classrooms. Fine trelliswork covered the veranda to the street so no one could look in. Toward the inside, I could look straight into the classroom through barred windows without glass. Back from recess, girls with long oiled black hair that fell down their backs in single braids now filled the room. Some worked quietly at their desks while others listened to an older nun sitting at the teacher's desk. A study in contrasts, I thought, as I gazed at the black silhouettes of the mostly Indian girls against the white uniforms, the white walls, and the white nun.

It filled me with excitement to be starting school in such a different environment, with girls so unlike myself.

We went directly to the Crescent shopping area in Steamer Point where my mother bought yards and yards of white material for our uniforms. We carried it to a nearby tailor who worked in a room that was wide open to the street. Putting a tape measure around our waists, around our chests, across our shoulders, and around our hips he took our measurements.

"People are staring at us," Anna said.

I was self-conscious about the tailor measuring across my budding breasts, barely visible to anyone but myself, yet I defiantly ignored the people watching me.

Within a few days, the tailor had all our uniforms ready. Sure that our dresses would be dirty by the end of each school day, my mother had the tailor make one uniform for each day of the week. In her opinion, it would have been more practical with any color but white.

We rode to school with four or five other missionary kids from the Scottish Mission. Our transportation was a small Fiat 500—the tiniest of cars. How there was room for us all is a mystery. Some stood with heads out the sunroof, two sat on the front seat and the rest on the tiny back seat. There were constant fights. The driver repeatedly begged us to behave or we would have an accident. One day when his pleas went unheard, he lost patience and cursed us:

"Your father's mother is a dog."

The streetwise *ayyal Bain*, the adopted children of the Scottish nurse, Miss Bain, hurled epithets back at him. In turning to physically calm us, he temporarily lost control of the car and barely avoided landing us in a salt pond by the road.

Though I was excited about the new school, I initially felt incompetent. My English was inadequate and the classroom situation confusing. The teacher taught two grades in the same room. Overwhelmed, I stared at the textbooks. There were pages and pages of geography and history I could barely read. To adequately prepare myself for classes I would have to mentally translate all lessons into Danish so I could understand them, then translate them back into English for retelling, but homework was hardly worth that much time. As a result, I was often unprepared. Like a deaf person hearing only every other word, I drew conclusions based on half-truths.

At home, I enjoyed popping into the kitchen to see Mustafa. His manner was easygoing and fatherly and I always felt welcomed by him. He enlisted my help in peeling bananas and oranges, slicing them to mix with other fruit.

Mustafa wore a long futa, and a shirt. He artfully folded a turban around his head. Of average height and very skinny, he had a concerned, caring, solicitous way about him that I loved.

The kitchen was large. We cleaned the dishes in big sinks and rinsed them with boiling water from a huge heated tank hanging from the ceiling. All food was cooked on kerosene stoves. Mustafa went to the market every day and came home with large baskets full of fruits, vegetables, and meats. My mother, with Mustafa's help, cooked Danish meals, but we had many exotic tropical fruits, most of which were new to Anna and me.

We ate in the large dining room. With its high ceilings, cement floors, and ceiling fan it was always cool. We dined at the large, solid oak table with heavy high-backed chairs. The "boy," Abdur-Rahman, flitted the room several times a week with a fine, pungent DDT mist to kill the cockroaches. This smell mingled with the aroma of the fruits we had for dessert: oranges, bananas, pomegranate, dates, papaw, and mango. I disliked the mango and in my mind, its turpentine-like taste was forever linked to the smell of DDT.

Despite the initial frustration at school, I was happy. Clad in shorts I played outside with Anna and the kids from the hospital compound. I climbed trees, circumscribed the compound balancing on the pitch of the six-foot-high mud wall, jumped off it into the sand dunes, and climbed on and off the roofs of the servants' quarters.

Our parents gave Anna and me black and white kittens. Mine was a Manx. I loved the fluffy, playful bundle. Stumpy I called him. Anna's was a female and the two kittens romped around the compound chasing each other into palm trees.

The monkey chained to the thorny acacia tree was neither playful nor friendly, I found out for myself. I wanted to hold and cuddle him, but he bit and pinched. I watched him, struck by his very human behavior. I talked to him, tried to lure him closer, but he threw pebbles and date kernels at me. The monkey was cranky and sad, it seemed.

You Can't Go Home Again

It was early morning. I was wide-awake; another school day lay ahead. Yet something was different this morning I soon realized. Intermittent stomach cramps had awakened me; I hoped they would go away soon so I could go to school. Staying home was too boring. As I was getting dressed, however, I found to my consternation that there was blood in my underwear. I heard my mother in our parents' bedroom and called to her as I rushed into the bathroom:

"Mum, come here."

My mother appeared in the door.

"Mum, what's happening? My stomach is cramping…I can't go to school." I showed her the underwear.

My mother looked at me, a little surprised, yet also apologetic.

"I should have prepared you for this," she said, "but I didn't expect it to happen so soon." She sat down on the edge of the bathtub.

"You didn't expect what to happen?" I asked. "You mean you knew this was going to happen?"

"Well, this is what happens to all girls when they get to be about thirteen or fourteen, when they start to develop into women. You are bleeding from the uterus—also called the womb; it is getting prepared for the babies you may have some day. Once a month for many years, you will have the same symptoms and signs."

I felt the pains again and thought: I can't believe that I'll have to go through this every month for years and years. I could care less about having babies sometime when I was a grown woman.

"Mum, I don't want this."

"Well, I'm afraid you have no choice." My mother was very matter-of-fact. "I'll help you fashion a pad from some rags and cotton wool so your panties don't get all bloody again." How disgusting, I thought.

Together we went into the bedroom. Fortunately my father and Anna had gone downstairs. My mother found some materials and quickly sewed up a pad for me.

"By the way this is not something you need talk about or complain about. It happens to every young girl and woman. You just have to accept it and put up with it," my mother said.

"Well, I'm sure not getting a lot of sympathy," I mumbled, feeling angry and sorry for myself. I felt betrayed by my mother and by my body.

I was only twelve years old. I didn't want to become a woman! I wanted to stay as I was, I thought; I wanted to remain a child. I loved to play and challenge myself with my friends. I thought about long days of carefree play in the house on Hans Egedesvej in Denmark. Forgetting all its drabness I suddenly became very lonesome for the world I had left behind.

As I got ready for school—yes, you *can* go to school, my mother had said giving me two aspirin —I thought of summers spent at my godparents' vicarage where in the long summer evenings we played until midnight. From the time I was nine until I was twelve, I had gone to stay with my godparents every summer. I loved the large old vicarage, I loved my aunt Lisbeth and uncle Lars, and I loved their five rambunctious boys. Invariably there was a pattern to my visits there; every year was the same. Those were the most beautiful and carefree times of my life.

I dawdled over breakfast, lost to my surroundings as I dwelled on the memory of my arrivals in that enchanted environment each summer when school let out.

Bo waits for me at the station in Sorø. He is a tall, blond, handsome boy, the middle of my godparents' five sons. He intimidates me somewhat; he is older than me by three years. Confident and good-looking, he loves to boss around his younger siblings, including me when I am there. He is also my guardian angel: when his younger brothers tease me, he defends me; when they refuse to play with me, he coaxes them into including me. Therefore, more than anything, I adore him.

He has come to the station in the gig. He heaves my luggage onto a seat. I jump through the small gate at the back of the gig and seat myself across from him. He pulls the reins, clicks his tongue, and away we go. I don't have much to tell Bo; anything I could tell him from home pales in comparison with his life. Instead, I sit quietly as the wind blows through my hair.

I think of the charmed existence my godfather's five boys lead. They go to school at the renowned Sorø Academy, an old institution in a park like setting near Sorø Lake. They bike the eight miles to school, through the beautiful countryside. In summer, they help in the vicarage and on the farm. They play in the woods and the fields; they fish, they swim. I envy them.

As the gig rolls along, I smell the wild flowers along the road, and the hay from nearby fields. In the woods, the sun filters through a canopy of beeches; light shimmers in my eyes. Then we are in open fields again, fields of oats, wheat, and barley and I know we are close. The road winds down a hill into Alsted village. I am full of anticipation. Sjørn, the tenant farmer at the vicarage, lives at the top of the hill. He is an old man who with his wife always welcomes me to their home. He lives in a cottage several centuries old, its thatched roof so low I can almost reach the lower part of it, its half-timbered walls crooked, the timbers painted red, the masonry white. The hollyhocks in front of the little house are flowering. Sjørn is in the vegetable garden hoeing the potatoes. I shout a greeting to him, but I can't stop to talk, I say. Dinner is waiting at the vicarage.

The road curves past the farms that for centuries have clustered in the village. In its center, at the highest point, stands the church, gleaming white, keeping watch over everything. Next to it is the vicarage. The horse knows the way home and brings the gig into the courtyard, around the huge, shady chestnut tree, and the circular bench surrounding it. It stops by the front door.

My godmother, aunt Lisbeth, a round woman, runs out, scoops me up into her arms, and gives me a hug. My godfather, pastor Lars Andersen, a tall studious man with glasses, appears behind her, beaming. I feel welcome. It overwhelms me that people outside my family care about me and love me.

There are so many things and places to explore. The boys' messy rooms; Uncle Lars's large, cozy study with its huge writing desk and book-case-lined walls; the piano room where I play almost daily; the quiet, intimate living room, with its horsehair chairs and sofas, where I curl up and read for hours; the huge dining room, the vital center of the vicarage, where the table is already set for dinner—twelve to twenty people eat here at any given meal; the kitchen with its old wood stove where aunt Lisbeth cooks up big meals with the help of the kitchen maid; and the pantry where the dishes, glasses, and silverware are kept, and where food is placed on serving platters before it is carried to the table. I run down the corridor at the east end of the house, past aunt and uncle's bedroom, past other bedrooms occupied by paying guests, to the very end of the hall where my bedroom is. It is so small it must have been a closet, the window so high I can't look out.

I am quite out of breath after my whirlwind tour through the house. I tell every room, every piece of furniture: "I'm back! I'm back!"

Then the gong sounds. It's time to eat. I stop in the bathroom to wash my hands. When I get to the dining room, I find the guests already seated at their assigned places. The five boys are the last to arrive. I sit next to Auntie. I pull out a starched linen napkin from a linen pouch with my name on it, and unfold it in my lap.

Uncle Lars says grace and the meal begins. Auntie expects good manners, and the boys and I pass the dishes to the paying guests first. Conversation is lively around the table. Among the paying guests are working or retired schoolteachers, nurses, librarians, pastors, professors, and doctors. The dinner conversations are about books read, music heard, sermons preached, politics, and the state of the country.

We eat huge country meals: chicken, pork or beef roasts, vegetables, potatoes, and gravy; and desserts: *frugtgrød* (fruit pudding), *æblekage* (apple crisp), *fløjlsgrød* (velvet pudding), and many others. I stuff myself; meals are never like this at home. After dinner, the boys and I help clear the table and wash the dishes.

It is midsummer and the evening is light until eleven. After the chores, I check out the garden. Hammocks connect tall, old maple, beech, and chestnut trees. I take refuge here during afternoon rest periods when children are seen but not heard. Here I read while flies and bees buzz and the wind rustles the leaves in the treetops. The gravel paths between the four lawns are raked in intricate patterns; huge tujas on the grass give off intoxicating resinous smells.

On the east side of the lawns, behind a hedge, are berry bushes, raspberries, black- and red currant, strawberries, and gooseberries and further down an orchard with apple trees, pears, cherries, and plums. When the fruit is ripe, Auntie will put us children to work picking them. The boys often anticipate this event and make themselves scarce, but aunt Lisbeth knows where to find them.

At the bottom of the garden, separated from it by another hedge, is the vegetable garden, rows and rows of potatoes, cabbage, peas, carrots, beets, and radishes. Beyond are fields of grain where the boys and I play and hide causing Sjørn fits of anger:

"Who has been trampling the oats?" We pretend to be innocent.

Later in the evening, I check the horse stables saying hello to every horse, rubbing their foreheads. I visit the few milking cows and their calves, enter the hen house where the chickens fly up and cackle. Auntie will send me here in the mornings to gather eggs, I know.

There is time for a game of croquet before bedtime. The croquet hoops are set on the lawn closest to the house. Uncle Lars and the boys induce some guests to play. The boys are skilled and competitive players and often win. I always lose.

The boys and I bring in the hay from the meadow. We ride back to the vicarage on top a fragrant load of grass and clover. I am at the reins feeling important, but I need do nothing, the horses know where to go. We start forking the hay into the loft, but soon forget our purpose. Jumping off the loft into the cart, we throw hay bales at each other. I love these fights. Soon hay and dust cover us; we are filthy and sweaty. Sjørn comes running across the yard breaking up this wildness:

"You better get on with forking that hay, or I'll have a word with the pastor."

No idle threat. The pastor is a strict disciplinarian, and God knows he needs to be.

We are by Susåen, a meandering stream in the meadows. We fish all day for carp, and swim in the lazy stream. I, used to the sand beaches of the ocean, dislike soppy grass and rushes. Nor do I like toads or grass snakes, but decide that if the boys can swim here, so can I.

Loving height and danger, we climb the tall pines along the driveway, daring each other higher and higher. From here, we can see all the way to the twin towers of Fjenneslev Kirke (Church). How well we know its story. Repeatedly uncle Lars, in his didactic, academic voice, lectures on Danish history at the dinner table. He loves to tell the legend of Fjenneslev Kirke: a famous, early-twelfth-century squire, Asser Rig, went away to war while his wife was expecting a child. Before leaving he extracted from her the promise that she would build a tower on the church if the child were a boy. On his return he saw from afar the twin towers announcing the birth of his twin sons Absalon and Esben Snare.

Alsted Kirke is a whitewashed church with a red tile roof. The gables of its single tower have a characteristic step-like pattern. A gate from the vicarage garden leads across a field path to a gate into the churchyard. Sunday mornings uncle Lars makes his way through the gates, sermon and Bible in hand, black gown swishing around his long legs, white ruff bobbing at his neck. It is an unspoken rule that everyone is to be at the service. The boys often defiantly declare they do not intend to go, but come straggling in at the last minute, hair unkempt, eyes filled with sleep.

Vast green lawns are my access to this memory. The sight of them conjures up images of wooden balls, clubs, croquet hoops, and an idyllic half-timbered house and I regain a lost time. I have recreated a memory of my godparents' vicarage that is so tangible it seems I can hold it in my hands, touch it and delight in it. I handle it gingerly, afraid of crushing it. I turn it and look at it from many sides. It is a thing of beauty and innocence, an innocence I can never retrieve. I take it out from time to time, I hold it lovingly, and it never changes.

At not quite thirteen, in Aden, I thought about this place with great longing. But I could not go home again to my school, my friends, and least of all to my godparents. It was not within my parents' means to allow that. I must stay here, in a society where girls marry at a young age and take on adult responsibilities, where girls cannot be children at age thirteen. I felt a little lost. I was no longer a child, yet I didn't belong in the world of adults. With no one to identify with, with no peers, I entered adolescence alone.

Fascination...and Jealousy

Living in an Arab country made our parents worry about us considerably. In some ways, it should have been easier than had we lived in Denmark. Aden had few worldly temptations and influences; Muslims don't dance and drink—issues that much concerned our parents—and Arab men are generally more respectful of women and girls than western men.

But our parents had us under close supervision. They gave us little freedom. They prohibited us from going to the market alone, and forbade us to walk the streets in town without an escort.

My mother now also wanted me to wear dresses instead of the khaki shorts I loved. It was more appropriate, she thought. Arabs took offense at a girl my age showing her legs. I was not happy; all of a sudden I was expected to behave like a much older person.

Despite all this, my disenchantment did eventually give way to the realization that I must accept what was happening to me; my parents could do nothing to change it.

I therefore greeted our move to The Manse as a welcome distraction when late in 1950 the Walkers returned from their home leave. The Manse was about a quarter of a mile away and here lived Dr. Raymond Smith, a bachelor missionary doctor.

Fortunately, I had at this time become increasingly fond of reading. I buried myself in books, escaping into another world. It was almost impossible to satisfy my hunger for reading. Once I read English with ease, I immersed myself in books about Arabia, books by explorers, books available at the Mission Book Store. They created in me the romantic notion of adventure among the Arabs. One of the American missionaries also brought me a number of Ruth Fielding books, the ongoing saga of a young American girl maturing into womanhood, written between 1913 and 1935; not great literature, they nonetheless helped me expand my vocabulary. The books I read were of Ruth at my age. Though her circumstances were different, I felt she experienced similar emotions.

While we lived at uncle Raymond's my mother was responsible for the household. It was not easy for her working with Dr. Smith's cook, however; he was in no way as amiable as Mustafa. He had his repertoire that he would rather stick with—menus much influenced by British cuisine. My mother liked making Danish food, and uncle Raymond seemed to enjoy it. Yet the cook continually raised objections and hated my mother's interference. She then realized that he had been making a nice income for himself before we moved in, overcharging uncle Raymond for foods bought in the market. As my mother was the ultimate thrifty saver she quickly caught on to the cook's tricks, and began doing all the shopping herself. She knew exactly how to drive a hard bargain. You didn't pay the price the merchants asked the first time around, nor the second or third. They raised their prices for the *nasrani*, or the *frangi* as they also called the whites, and my mother was not about to pay those prices. She knew how to walk away until the merchant offered a price she was willing to pay.

When living at The Manse we now rode to school with Stella and Lily, the daughters of the Greek owner of the Salt Works; our father brought us there in the morning and picked us up again in the afternoon. At times Anna stayed to play with the Greek girls.

I had no time for my little sister and her friends. I had other interests. I had taken a fancy to a cousin of uncle Raymond's, Derek Bray, a captain in the Royal Air Force who now was close to finishing his tour of duty. My entire family enjoyed his company, but he particularly lavished attention on me. He had often come to dinner at Kintore and came even more frequently at The Manse. His presence significantly brightened life for me and I hung on his every word. He often put his arms around me and held me. He was thirty and I was thirteen and he most likely—one would hope—meant this as a brotherly gesture, but it fueled fires and longings in me, lonely and peerless as I was. He was the organist at the Presbyterian Church in Steamer Point that we attended, and before leaving he explained the organ to me and asked if I would take over his job when he went back to England. He treated me as someone his own age, which was very empowering, but also very seductive.

I was devastated when he returned to Britain, leaving me with the promise that he would write. He lived up to his word and for a time I lived for his letters, treasuring them and frequently rereading them.

Uncle Raymond was likewise a person both Anna and I adored. Sometimes he took us for joyrides into the desert in his Land Rover. An especially exciting trip was the day Auntie Pat had agreed to marry uncle Raymond. Pat was a missionary in Ethiopia and via mail, she had said yes to his proposal. He was so ecstatic that he took us for a ride. Driving up and down the sand dunes he sang—out of tune and at the top of his lungs—"My Bonnie lies over the ocean, and my Bonnie lies over the sea…."

We often went to the mission compound with him. Though we lived less than a mile from the compound where our friends were, my mother wouldn't dream of letting us walk there. Not only was it too hot to walk, but also it was not safe: the desert road was not well traveled.

On that road from the mission hospital, my mother one day behaved abominably toward our father for reasons we did not understand—yet, we were quick to take our father's side. Our mother was so consumed with anger and jealousy that she asked our father to stop the car, while she stormed out, slamming the door after her, declaring that she would walk home. Whatever possessed her? Later we learned that shortly before my father had talked to Miss Bain, one of the Scottish missionary nurses; he had leaned out his car window, his smile debonair and his tone gentle and courteous, as the two of them talked about a picnic for the children the following week. My mother, however, often saw only flirtatiousness in the friendly smiles my father bestowed on women, especially if they were single women as Miss Bain. Never mind that she was a devoted missionary nurse who had adopted three orphans, one Arab, one Jewish, and one Somali.

How difficult it must have been for my mother to experience and control those feelings.

My mother was happy, though, that I visited the hospital with uncle Raymond. She was hoping I would fulfill her ambition for me to become a doctor. She had entertained that hope for each of my older siblings in turn, but none had shown an interest. My mother hoped that I some day would return to Aden as a medical missionary. Yet, she was realistic in worrying that it might be impossible to continue the mission work once Aden became independent. By now it was certain that that would happen some time in the not so distant future.

A Medical Adventure

I was peering into the relative darkness of the clinic where uncle Raymond was seeing patients. We were upcountry—in the interior of the Protectorate. My family and I were accompanying uncle Raymond on his trip to visit the Mission's clinics. I stood quiet and wide-eyed at the door observing the people. I saw little children with chubby cheeks and large round bellies, their arms and legs like sticks, crowding around their mothers. One little girl was crying and reaching for consolation at her mother's breast, tugging at it, but the mother pushed her away and offered the tired, floppy breast to the emaciated infant she held in her arms. Old men squatted along the walls, some ghostly pale, others so thin their knees protruded like knobs under their thin skin. Older children stared at me with curiosity, their eyes matted with infection: trachoma, a disease that if untreated would eventually blind them. Inside the door sat a young man who was in the process of stripping off a dirty dressing from a huge, penetrating, festering sore on his shin.

We had left Aden the day before, in a lorry and a Land Rover, both filled with supplies. Several Bedouins hitched a ride on the lorry where they clung to its sides. We first traveled along bumpy tracks that led toward the Gulf of Aden. The tracks were faint and as my eyes followed them across the desert, I could not help but think of Wilfred Thesiger who decades before had traveled across the part of the Arabian desert called *Rub'-al-Qali*—the Empty Quarter—on camel back. I was busy reading about the explorers of Arabia and Thesiger's book *Arabian Sands* had been a recent read. The Bedouins who had accompanied him had found their way through the unmarked desert by following signs in the sand only they could divine. The tracks of our lorry and Land Rover were so faint they would disappear in a sandstorm and I wondered if the medical team ever got lost. Maybe they should rely on Bedouins to help them.

When we reached the beach, we drove on a wide moist stretch of ocean sand. I tasted and smelled the salty, iodine spray from waves crashing on the beach. It was so hot and the ocean looked so inviting that I wanted to go swimming, but "no," uncle Raymond said, "we need to press on. We'll stop later."

We passed little villages consisting of shacks made of sticks and burlap. The women of the village, shifting half-naked toddlers from one hip to the other, watched us go by. They wore no veils, their dresses were tattered, and faded kerchiefs covered their hair. The men, in gray, worn loincloths were unfolding their nets and preparing to fish. At the periphery of the village small black and white goats hopped from sand dune to sand dune, nibbling away at the bushes. Older children, similarly near naked, their hair light and brittle, wiped drainage from inflamed eyes as they waved.

I magnanimously returned their greeting. I was fatalistic about the poverty surrounding me. That my family and I, and other whites like us, ate well and lived comfortably while others lacked all basic comforts and often did not have enough to eat, gave me little pause for thought.

We stopped in Shuqra for the night, a seaside market town consisting of solid mud houses. At a primitive guesthouse close to the water's edge, my mother prepared dinner on a kerosene stove while the rest of us, hot and dirty, swam in the ocean. Refreshed, we hungrily devoured my mother's simple meal before settling into bed.

In the morning, the sun rose huge and red out of the Indian Ocean, growing smaller as it climbed into a cloudless sky. We headed inland and arrived an hour later at our first destination, the village of Gi'ar. The area was lush; fertile fields, irrigated by intermittent rivers, surrounded the village. The convoy stopped at the clinic whose whitewashed mud brick walls gleamed brightly among the brown mud houses.

Uncle Raymond was tall, gangly, and boyish looking. He had a long, bony face and a thatch of brown hair, tamed by Brylcreme. He invited me inside the clinic. Following him around I watched him as he saw patient after patient. He had a nervous intensity about him; it seemed he never stood still.

As he examined the patients, I watched concerned family members surrounding them, small children showing apprehension as uncle Raymond examined their mothers, and older people fearing his verdict. He treated them and reassured them, and I became aware of how grateful the patients were as they repeated: "*Shukran, shukran*, (thank you, thank you) and *Al-hamd-u-lil-lah* (thanks be to God)." These people had the same concerns as my family and I had; families cared for them and feared losing them. The clinic gave patients hope of healing, yet uncle Raymond was quick to point out that not all could be helped, their disease was too advanced, their nutrition too poor. My thoughts went to my mother who now had recovered from her amoebic dysentery. Was it possible that she could have died? The mere thought of that overwhelmed me.

Yet it was hard for me to put myself in their place. Because they were so poor, because they experienced death at every turn, I somehow felt that they looked at life differently, that they were more accepting of their fate. My thoughts about their attitude puzzled me and left me without answers.

The convoy made its way up from the plains. We crossed one swollen waterway after another, crossing the larger rivers at fords because there were no bridges. Water splashed up around the wheels and the vehicles became covered in mud. In the back of the Land Rover Anna and I, dirty and dusty, were baked by the sun.

We traveled between millet fields whose tall, healthy corn wafted over our heads. Green leaves engulfed us and we had no sense of where we were going. We smiled and waved at a shepherd boy who stood at the side of the road, a flock of goats surrounding him. After we passed, the boy moved the goats forward toward the village. With exaggerated gestures, showing off because of us, he urged the stragglers on.

The road climbed over long stretches of hardened lava. The heat reflected off the rocks and the afternoon sun scorched our legs through the back opening. We were tired now and ready to be at our destination. I wished the day were over. So much had happened and I did not know how to interpret it all. How could uncle Raymond stand doing this job day in and day out? He must be exhausted, yet I also saw how grateful many patients were. Just the possibility of being cured, or even of just getting better, made them thankful to uncle Raymond and to God. *Shukran* and *Al-hamdu-lillah* they said, putting their palms together as they looked up at the white doctor and toward heaven.

I saw the government fort in Mudia from afar. A large white building, built from dark volcanic rock and white mortar, it stood apart from the village. Parapets graced its top and through small loopholes at the first- and third story levels soldiers could scan the countryside for enemies and open fire if necessary.

Native soldiers in British employ welcomed us and showed us to our accommodations in one of the towers.

I fell asleep on my army cot under the protective mosquito net, and dreamt of all the sick people I saw that morning. So many of them were at death's door, but in the dream, they all walked away healed.

The next day I decided I had enough of sick people. I also had no desire to be with my parents as they talked to people about God. They would have a small service at the clinic before the day started and they would follow up by talking to patients in the waiting room. I had something quite different in mind that day and was happy my parents were occupied.

"Ya, Muswad, oh Muswad, how about showing me how to drive?" I said to the driver of the lorry.

"No way," Muswad laughed, "this is the Sahib's lorry...."

"*Min fadlak, ya Muswad*, oh Muswad, please...I'm sure that I can learn how to do that."

He shook his head in disbelief. I knew what he was thinking: What's with her? She always thinks she can do everything.

"You're a girl, a child," he said. "You should not be driving."

"But I would like to learn how to. Please..."

After more cajoling Muswad relented. I saw this as the perfect place to learn, in this distant village, outside law and order, surrounded by wide-open spaces. There was no need to worry about staying on a road. There was none, just the desert.

Soon I was at the wheel trying to master the clutch of the heavy old lorry. It moved forward in fits and starts and stalled as the engine died. I started it up again; it moved; it stalled. I repeated this until the lorry finally moved forward. This was heady stuff, I thought. I was excited, yet I knew I had to be careful or Muswad would never forgive me and would certainly never again allow me behind the wheel. Slowly I drove away from the outskirts of the village and into the desert. All I had to watch for were the goats and…oh, yes, the donkeys! Soon I got the hang of it. I drove and drove.

Muswad initially was quite anxious and cautioned me repeatedly to be careful, but after a while, he relaxed a little.

When finally back at the Fort, I could barely contain my excitement and now that it was over Muswad was almost as excited as I was. When later I sought out my parents and confronted them with the news, my father just laughed and shook his head, but my mother, who had never learned to drive, took it more seriously.

"Oh, Martha, what were you thinking of. You could have hurt someone or run into something."

"But I didn't, Mummy, I drove just fine."

Later in the day, Anna and I set off to explore the village in the company of one of the soldiers whose uniform had none of the starched crispness of his British counterparts. Under a dirty khaki shirt, he wore just a loincloth; on his head a khaki turban, one end of which trailed down his back; on his feet leather sandals. He followed us wherever we went, a rifle over his shoulder.

Here all men of standing, and not just the soldiers, carried guns. They also carried a *gambiyya*—a double-edged, wide, curved, short knife—and a cartridge belt around their waists. I walked with the soldier at my side and it didn't occur to me to fear these fierce looking men. Instead, I thought they looked proud and handsome with their fine features and prominent cheekbones, their indigo dyed skin and shoulder length hair, and with the *mushadda* wound around their heads. I could not imagine any of them hurting me. I knew there was and had been fighting among the tribes since time immemorial, but that violence should be directed at us was inconceivable. I had the notion that the Arabs loved us.

The women eyed Anna and me cautiously from doorways or through the open shutters. Only an old woman was not afraid to show her amazement at the two white apparitions. I didn't understand her dialect, but the soldier interpreted as the old woman made little clucking noises, touched our blond hair, and pinched our arms. She smiled and turned to the other women:

"Now—would you believe this?"

The soldier teased her.

"*Ya 'agooza*—oh, old woman- have you never seen a white person before?" She shook her head and laughed aloud. I, however, had questions of my own.

"How come you have those trains at the back of your dresses?" I asked.

The woman whispered, shy and as if imparting a great secret:

"Oh, we have to wipe out our footsteps in the sand so no evil man or spirit can follow us."

A soldier gave us a gazelle that was only a few days old. Insecure and wobbly it stood on its spindly legs, barely a foot tall. We adored it and over the next couple of days, we took care of it as best we could. We tried to make it drink powdered milk and water; we combed the countryside for greens to feed it. Yet, it got weaker and weaker. If only we had a nursing bottle, we thought, then we could get it to drink more. However, the gazelle crumbled into a small heap, its tiny front legs splayed out in front of it. No matter how much we encouraged it, we were unable to make it feed or drink anymore, and finally it died. We buried it in the desert.

One day we walked near the mountains. A seductive plaint of quartertones, repetitive and limited in range, commanded our attention. We saw a small shepherd boy leading his sheep down the mountain toward us, blowing on a flute made out of a reed. The simple melody gathered the sheep behind him. Before he reached us, he stopped and picked up something. He was totally unaffected and unsurprised by our presence. He handed me a tiny lizard that fit easily into the hollow of my hand. It crawled up my thumb, its tiny claws clinging to my skin, its tongue lashing out at some perceived food object.

"*Shukran*," I said.

The shepherd boy smiled, happy that this small gift pleased me. He was skinny, his legs depigmented and deformed, his loincloth faded, and, over his shoulders, he wore a shawl that retained some indigo color. He seemed so fragile.

I wondered if he was sick.

I enjoyed the lizard. I kept it in a matchbox and, guarding it zealously, I fed it what I thought it might like, green leaves from the desert scrub. It also died.

As we drove back to Aden I thought about all my experiences. I was gleeful that I had learned to drive, but then the thought of the sick people, and the dead gazelle, and even the dead lizard, put me in a more somber mood. It was hard to live here, I thought, it was so easy to die. I wondered if the shepherd boy also would die. Who decided who was to live and who was to die? Of course God did, I was sure. Yet, why did He allow Arabs to die more readily than white people? I understood that white people were stronger because their nutrition was better, because they got treatment when they became sick, but then why did everything good happen to them? Surely, it was not just chance. No, God decided these things, I thought, and there must be some purpose to God's plan.

Or was there?

Persecution

Aden is a frightful rock without a single blade of grass
or drop of fresh water...I am like a prisoner here.
— ARTHUR RIMBAUD, AGE 26 (1880)

My mother was getting dinner ready. The kerosene stove was causing her problems.

"Oh, I will get it going for you, *ya Sitt* (oh, lady)," Abdullah said. "I know how to do this," but she said no; she would do it herself; she didn't trust he really knew. Finally, it was lit and she could start her pressure cooker. My mother found this a very convenient invention, particularly in this country. However tough the meat, the pressure cooker would get it tender. For dessert she had Abdullah slice up the fruit she bought in the market, most of it imported from across the Red Sea.

After a year-and-a-half in Sheikh Othman—the last six months at The Manse—we had finally moved to Crater and my father was working for the Danish Mission. My mother now helped at the Danish Mission's Arab Girls' School, which had moved to a new, just completed building in Crater. It was light and airy and had a large outdoor space surrounded by a high wall where the girls could play during physical education and recess. It was at the edge of the city toward the mountains. My father drove her to the school every morning. She had the youngest girls for arithmetic and was grateful to be teaching again. There had been a shift in people's attitudes toward the education of girls since she was last here, she realized. Increasing numbers of fathers wanted their girls to learn to read and write. As the government girls' school could not accommodate everyone, many fathers resorted to sending their girls to the Mission School where they were aware the girls would learn about Christ. My mother thanked God for every opportunity to plant a seed.

My father was busy evangelizing and he also helped Mubarak at the bookstore, which had grown and expanded. It had not only Arabic literature, but much English as well; in fact it was the only English language bookstore in the whole colony. Mubarak, their faithful and *only* Christian convert, was slow and methodical—perfect for the bookstore—but in great need of help.

My mother was pleased to be living at Hebron, a new house built for Danish missionary families. When she had been pregnant with me they had lived in a rambling old house close to Sira Island; the house was big and impractical and they had needed many servants. Hebron was modern and attractive, but without the spaciousness and high ceilings of the old colonial home and certainly not intended for a large family. It had two bedrooms and a bathroom upstairs, a large room below that served as both dining and living room, verandas on both sides; on the east side, part of the veranda was made into an office. An attached building at the back housed a conference room and Abdullah's room and bathroom.

Though she had enjoyed living at The Manse and taking care of the bachelor Raymond Smith my mother was happy finally having a house of her own. She was likewise happy that the house was small enough that she did not need many servants. Her motto had always been: a penny saved is a penny earned, so not having many servants suited her fine. She managed quite well with our "boy" Abdullah's help, and I was entrusted with ironing all our clothes now that we had an electric iron; my mother wouldn't have trusted me with a flat iron and red-hot coals. The only other help we had was a woman who came in to do the laundry for us a couple of days a week.

Every Wednesday night, my father had the Young Men's Club. In a mission magazine he once told a story about an evening at the Club. Having often been with him to the Club and knowing what the scenes in the street usually were like, I can well imagine how his evening passed.

My father arrives at Beit-ash-Sharif after having eaten dinner at home. He parks his little black Ford Anglia outside. The street is filled with people, light bulbs dangle from the ceiling in the small stalls across the street; a neon light casts its blue-white shadows on the broken blacktop. Young boys gather around his car.

"*Masa' el-kheir*" (good evening), he says quietly and looks up at them with a diffident smile, "*keif halekum?*" (how are you?). He knows he doesn't exude confidence, because he isn't confident. It is never safe being in the streets alone at night. Many of the young boys approach him aggressively.

"So what are you going to do tonight? Tell us stories about the Messiah or what?" He confirms that he will and he invites them to come inside in a little while and listen. Listen to him talking, and listen to music. Their laughter is derisive, and one of them raps on the hood with a stick, breaking into drum rhythms, quietly at first, then with a menacing intensity. Angry, my father feels his face getting red. He controls himself and quietly and deliberately he says:

"Please stop that."

The boy stops abruptly, taken aback by the white man's quiet anger. He walks away squinting at my father, teeth clenched.

My father looks up at the building. All the shutters are closed, as are the double doors in the lower part. The house is dark. Jack isn't home, he thinks. Maybe he, Kathleen, and the boys went to the beach before sunset and haven't returned yet? He doesn't want to open the club until Jack gets there. It is easier when they are two. He opens the front door, turns on the bulb in the stairwell, goes to the second floor, flips on the light switch, and throws open the shutters to let in the cool night air. He goes to the kitchen. On plates he arranges the biscuits and cookies he has brought and everything is ready for tea when Jack walks in.

"I'm sorry I'm late. As you know, Kathleen is not feeling strong, so we walked slowly. I am glad you are here and have gotten things started."

Jack puts on a record while my father arranges the tables in the front room. He goes down into the street and invites the boys and young men gathered there inside. Many come upstairs, some sit down at the tables and are soon absorbed in chess games. Others take books off the shelves and sit down to read. One young man has read most of a book and wants to finish it tonight. Others go into the room next door to play table tennis. In a third room, my father shows slides from the Holy Land and talks about Jesus' life. The young men have many questions. Most are aimed at testing the discrepancies between the Bible and the Qur'an. My father answers the questions calmly and asks questions back. He asks the young men what they believe about Jesus. "Was he a Prophet?"

"Yes, but one in a line of many, the last of whom was Mohammed."

"We believe He is God's Son," my father says, "He came to save us from sin."

"He can't be God's son. God has Prophets, but no sons."

My father pursues the discussion and reads to them from the Bible. The young men are polite and listen carefully. My father feels calm now and enjoys himself. He likes these young men and their very open and sincere questions. Here inside the Mission's building his confidence returns. He is meeting these young men on his own territory.

Other young men don't get involved in the discussion, but stick to the games and books, or sit talking among themselves. Jack goes around and strikes up conversations. Jack's command of Arabic is tentative and he communicates with the boys on a very basic level, talking about Christ, offering scripture pamphlets. Jack is passionate about his calling, and wants to grasp every opportunity to witness about the Lord.

The evening passes quietly. My father and Jack are happy sharing the Gospel. Suddenly a loud noise shatters the night. My father rushes to the front room to see what has happened. A large rock lies on the floor. It has gouged a hole in the opposite wall. My father looks around.

"No one was hurt," a young man says. "It's just hooligans in the street; you have to forgive them."

My father smiles and thinks: That may be so, but there are also people who hate me and want to drive me out of here. He remembers when he had these meetings downstairs in the meeting hall. Young boys caused severe disruption. As soon as lights went out for slide shows the boys began booing and whistling, causing so much noise my father could barely make himself heard. All evening they drifted in and out of the hall howling like wild animals. My father in everything was a very controlled man and rarely did he lose his temper, but this tested him sorely. One night a fist-sized rock was thrown at him and narrowly missed his head. He was frightened, but managed to keep his equanimity, appearing serene on the outside while quaking within. Later one of the adults asked him:

"Where do you find the patience to deal with this?"

He answered:

"In God."

He knew he had to continue the meeting and not let fear take over. Besides, his anger with the boys steeled him. He prayed for patience so he wouldn't lose his temper. A loss of temper would surely cause the harassment to accelerate, he had felt. He continued with the same calm with which he had begun the meeting.

This Wednesday night the evening draws to a calm close. My father brings out the tea and biscuits and serves them to the young men. His announcement that he will end the evening with devotions causes an exodus. Many of the young men will not participate in Christian prayer. My father finishes with thanks to God who has brought them together on this night.

Jack and he close up the place after the men have left, sweeping the floors, washing the cups and dishes. When my father prepares to leave, he encounters a smell of urine in the stairwell. The light shows him where people—again young hooligans, he thinks—have urinated on the stairs. He fills a bucket with water and soap and washes the stairs. He finds the Ford Anglia covered with graffiti, written in the dust covering the car. He brushes across it, gets into the car, and drives home.

My father's days and nights were often like this and I wonder how he had the strength to continue his work. The following is another experience he wrote about:

My father goes into the streets around the market as he so often does. It is a busy place filled with people, men doing the shopping for the family, men sitting around talking, chewing qat, discussing important matters of the day. Few women are in the street, mostly older women, covered in the chador.

My father enters stores and coffee houses, talking to people, and selling pamphlets. This is usually a draining experience. The heat and the threatening situations he often encounters, take everything out of him.

In those back alleys, he stands out; a white man in drab khaki garb, he contrasts sharply with the colorful Arabs. Wherever he appears he is greeted with this defamation: "*Anta al-mughawwi*"—you are the seducer, the one who leads us astray. Often he is able to give out pamphlets without being harassed. People quietly accept them and some even pay for them while he talks to them.

That day a dignified older Arab man, wearing a white turban, a white shirt, and a long brightly colored futa, approaches my father, asks to buy two gospels from him, and pays for them. Then he takes out a cigarette lighter and sets the Gospels on fire.

"These are the seducer's books," he then shouts to the crowd. "We are good Muslims, and we should not allow this man to entice us to read these books. They are taboo to us."

The crowd cheers as the man holds the burning books up to them. As the books continue to burn, he dumps them on the ground. People throng around the man, and my father begins to feel the crowd closing in on him, crushing him on all sides. He fights to contain his fear. Many in the crowd begin threatening violence toward anyone who dares buy a gospel. My father retreats, burrowing through the mass of people. Once he gets to the outside of the crowd he has some breathing space; nonetheless, a large group follows him out into the alley, shouting epithets after him. Discouraged, he walks as quickly as he can to Beit-ash-sharif where his car is parked. In no time, he scales the steps to Jack's apartment on the third floor of the building. Jack welcomes him and they sit down to talk.

"I was once stoned in the same place," Jack says laughing, "but I am in good company. Just think what happened to Paul; he was almost killed."

As always, his friend, who glories in persecution, amazes my father.

❂

An Object of Desire

Hello, where you come from?"

The young Italian sailor painting the cabins on the foredeck smiled at me across his shoulder. It was early morning and I was exploring the ship. My family and I were on our way to Ethiopia; the heat of summer in Aden wore us down, and each year we spent a month or more in a milder climate. We had boarded the Italian freighter the night before and were now in the middle of the Gulf of Aden on our way to Djibouti. The sea was calm; already the sun was hot. We had slept on deck that night, in dilapidated deck chairs, and had woken early, stiff and disheveled, to contemplate the state of the ship. The hull was rusty, the paint on the bridge peeling, and the lifeboats in a state of disrepair. It was not reassuring and we prayed for safe passage.

I found myself alone on the foredeck with the sailor. Undisturbed by my presence he continued painting. With casual indifference he applied thick, white paint to the rusty, uneven, oft-painted surface, a cigarette hanging from the corner of his mouth. I barely understood his broken English.

"Your hair…beautiful…blond. Yes?"

I didn't move. I looked at him perplexed. I didn't quite know what to make of this man. He was swarthy, dressed in tattered pants, his upper body bare, his muscles taut. No one had ever commented on my hair; it was ordinary, dishwater blond. Nonetheless, I was flattered and curious. I looked around—up to the bridge—no one was around. The sailor put down his brush. With deliberate motions, he removed the cigarette from his mouth and dropped the ashes on deck. He now turned his full attention to me. I did not remember any one ever looking at me this way.

"And your eyes…"

The sailor moved across the deck—a slight swaying in his hips—and plant-ed himself close to me. The muscles of his shoulders and upper arm, and the tattoo on his forearm were inches from my face. His stale cigarette breath and the smell of his sweaty sunburned body assaulted me. I stepped away from him, but he stepped closer and I was now up against the railing. He smiled, a smile that made me uneasy. What did he want?

"Let me see your eyes…look at me."

He curled his right index finger under my chin and lifted my face toward his. Slowly I looked up. His black hair, tousled and streaked with paint, was combed back from his forehead; on the side of his cheek was a festering sore the size of a penny. His smiling eyes looked right into mine. They were filled with a meaning I didn't understand, something inappropriate, something forbidden. Somehow, I felt naked.

Suddenly everything about him became repulsive. I looked down and pulled my face away from his hand. I wrested myself free of the left arm he had placed around my shoulder and dodging under his right arm I started running.

"So…you don't like me, eh? I like you, why not stay here? Why you afraid?"

I ran as fast as my legs could carry me, around to the side of the ship… and stopped. My heart was beating and I was out of breath. I leaned over the railing and looked down at the water. I tried to slow my breathing. Why had I run? I should just have talked to him and asked him to remove his hands so I could have walked away in a more dignified manner. But what would he have done; what could he have done? He was much stronger than I. Could he have hurt me? I felt grateful my mother was nowhere in sight. How would I have explained this to her? My mother would be upset and worried.

I was now fourteen. The British young men I knew in Aden treated me with an innocent flirtatiousness and Arabs, if they looked at me at all, quickly averted their gaze. Since entering puberty, I had had an intense interest in the young RAF men I met at church; they preoccupied me and fascinated me. Yet this man was nothing like them. Standing at the railing, I pon-dered what had happened. Was this my mother's warned-of male animal lust? Could the sore in his face be due to syphilis? I had no answers and I did not want to discuss this with my mother, much less my father.

I stayed close to my family for the rest of the voyage.

Late in the afternoon, we arrived in Djibouti, a run-down colonial seaport, in the tiny colony of French Somaliland. The French appeared to have no compunction at the lack of maintenance of their government houses, streets, and gardens. I found everything depressing and squalid as we drove through town in a cab. The houses were dilapidated; even homes obviously belonging to the French had chipped stucco and crumbling garden walls. The streets were all potholes; sewage and garbage filled the gutters.

We arrived at the run-down, brown, wooden house belonging to Mr. André Trombettas, my father's Greek friend, one of many expatriate merchants from countries in the Mediterranean, Middle East, Yemen, and India who had and continue to set up shop along the sea routes to India and Africa. Often they spend their entire lives in voluntary exile, supporting their families.

His house was locked and empty. We had dismissed the cab and we now found ourselves alone on the sidewalk with our luggage, wondering what to do next. The sun had set and darkness was falling. I felt conspicuous and vulnerable. A group of Somali women, beautiful, gaudy, and provocative in dress, passed us. The women were loud and friendly; they laughed and smirked, but my mother turned away in disgust.

"I think I had better go to Mr. Trombettas's store and get the key for the house," my father said.

I thought to myself: three white females alone on a sidewalk in this squalid part of town was inviting trouble. How could my father think we could be safe? But I knew my father did not see it this way. God was watching over us. And of course we were staying with friends, because that is what missionaries do. They do not waste money on hotels.

I sat down on my suitcase. The incident on the boat had made me watchful of all strange males. Somali men in dirty European garb continuously passed by and cast furtive glances at us. I felt more vulnerable than either Anna who was a child or my mother who was old.

When my father returned with Mr. Trombettas who had now closed up his shop, it had turned very dark; there were few streetlights and no moon. Mr. Trombettas was a rotund man with thinning hair, and beads of sweat formed little rivers trickling down his chubby cheeks. His shirt was drenched, his clothes dirty. It appeared he lived alone in this large, rambling, dark house with few creature comforts. The closed shutters kept out the light.

"My wife and children are in Greece, you know." Mr. Trombettas' English was poor.

The house hardly looked inhabited. Mr. Trombettas spent little time there; he was too busy in his store.

He showed us to our room. Mattresses covered the floor. Exhausted we gratefully prepared for bed. Yet, I was uneasy. Despite my father's reassurances that Mr. Trombettas was a good person, I didn't trust him. No European dressed that sloppily.

We suffered through the night; the heat, the humidity, the noises from the street, and the continuous whirring of mosquitoes were unbearable and disturbed our sleep. Yet, after a shower and a bountiful breakfast, prepared and served by a Somali woman who cooked for Mr. Trombettas, we felt better.

We had hoped to depart on the train for Dire Dawa in Ethiopia that morning, but couldn't leave. The police had confiscated our passports on arrival and had yet to return them. This city was threatening, I thought, one can't even trust the police. Yet I came to realize that Mr. Trombettas was indeed a good person; he continued to house and feed us; he went with us to the Police Station where he put pressure on the officers to return us our passports.

Two days later, we departed on an evening train filled with indigenous people all of whose possessions—bundles of clothes and firewood, chickens and goats—were packed into the car. The stench was intense.

We secured two wooden benches. My father read aloud a chapter from *Jungle Doctor*. I did not listen; I paid more attention to what was going on in the car. On all sides were locals, guileless people among whom I felt safe, poor people, people with dignity who didn't look to exploit every European.

Soon everyone settled down. Men and women, preparing for the night, wrapped themselves in enormous lengths of cloth and curled up on benches and floors. The hens stopped bickering, and even the goats lay down. Finally, we too went to sleep, taking turns lying on the benches.

On arrival in Dire-Dawa the next morning I stepped off the train and cool air, fresh and fragrant with rain, struck my face. The sordidness of the lowlands, the smells, the inappropriate leering of the Italian sailor, all were washed away in the downpour. How gloriously beautiful it was here.

A local bus took us over the Ahmar mountains to Harrar. The road was unpaved; sharp drop-offs at every turn frightened my mother but exhilarated Anna and me. My father again talked about his ill-fated attempts to be the good Samaritan on this very road many years before.

Our guest hut at the Swedish Mission in Harrar was light and airy. In a white blur, mosquito nets hung from the ceiling, falling in gentle pleats to the floor, enveloping the beds. The hut smelled of DDT, brown soap, and the scent from fruit trees outside. The front verandah was covered with bougainvillea. Our hosts, a Swedish missionary couple and their two young children, were welcoming and friendly. In the mornings I studied German; during the afternoons my father took Anna and me on long leisurely walks in the countryside; and at night he read aloud to our mother and us. Our days were tranquil and relaxed.

How different from the squalor of Djibouti, I thought. My experiences there and on the boat remained but bad memories. When I now think about Djibouti I cannot but wonder about colonial influence. Would Djibouti have been without its squalor had the French not been there? What was Africa like before the white people came? People in the countryside seemed different from the people in the urban areas. Had greed and hunger for the white man's world corrupted the latter? As a child in Africa I think I had the idea that the Europeans were doing something great by bringing western civilization to these backward countries. But it is futile to think of how things would have been had colonization not occurred. There is no way of knowing. As a child I also believed that the missionaries brought hope and salvation, but did that mean all of western civilization was desirable?

All too soon, our vacation was over and at the end of six weeks we faced the return trip. But now that we were rested and refreshed, we felt we were ready to tackle Djibouti again.

Where Will This Lead Me?

I woke up and slipped out the door onto the veranda whose concrete floor was still warm from yesterday's heat. From our home in Crater, I looked out at the ocean and breathed in the cool morning air. As I became awake, the sun rose out of the ocean into the pink candyfloss of clouds hovering near the horizon. The windows and the wooden shutters had been wide open all night and light breezes had cooled the room I shared with Anna, but now I closed them. After a quick bath, I dressed in a cool, clean, newly ironed, white school uniform.

"Good morning, Dad." My father was already in his study. "You're up early."

"I was awake and I thought I would start Sunday's sermon while it was still cool." He rose to join me at the table; he often suffered from insomnia.

Abdullah had breakfast ready for us: toast, eggs, fruit, tea, and reconstituted dry milk. When the four of us finished our meal Abdullah joined us for devotions. I looked over at him as he sat down. He was grinning widely and winking at me.

He was always so full of good humor, I thought happily. Abdullah was our "boy" and I just loved him. The British term "boy" grates on me as I write it. A "boy" was someone who helped the cook and he could be any age. But Abdullah was a boy. He was my age and had come to us from upcountry. His parents had sent him to Aden to earn money since they no longer could afford to feed him, and though the wage he was paid as a "boy" was small, he was able to help support his peasant family.

Abdullah was like a brother to Anna and me; we kidded each other, joked, and had fun together. As Abdullah spoke little English, the devo-

tions were in Arabic. Every morning we read a biblical text, each taking
turn reading a verse. Abdullah and I were both learning to read Arabic. As
we knew the Arabic alphabet we could read the text—Arabic is a phonetic
language—but neither of us was very fluent. Abdullah understood most of
what he read. I often understood little, but as my father explained the text, I
learned new words every day. Afterward my father prayed for God's guidance
throughout the day, for our siblings back in Denmark, for us, for the other
missionaries, and for the entire Arab world that they might get to know
Christ. We ended by saying the Lord's Prayer, in Arabic and in unison; even
Abdullah knew it by now.

As we took the dishes back to the kitchen, Abdullah whispered to me:
"So—we are praying for all the Arabs. That's good. The Arabs are good
people!" He played the buffoon, he was joking, but his sarcasm didn't escape
me. He was making fun of my parents' religion and that offended me. My
parents were so much in earnest about what they were doing. Bringing the
Gospel to the Arabs was the focus of their lives. So how could Abdullah
mock them?

I now wonder what importance his own religion played in his life and if he
went to the mosque regularly. Once he came home and said he had been to
the mosque. "You know our Prophet Muhammad—Peace be upon Him—
was a very Great Man!" and there was a strange gravity about him.

Anna and I were both in our uniforms and ready at the gate when the Haq's
car rolled up. We now rode to school with a Muslim Indian schoolmate. My
mother had searched high and low for a ride for us. The first several days after moving to Crater, we had either taken a bus-taxi or my father had driven
us to school. My father didn't have the time, however, and my mother didn't
like the taxi solution. First it cost money, though not much—but my mother
saved wherever she could; secondly, she didn't feel that we were safe riding
in the taxi, though I wondered what could possibly happen to us during a
six-mile ride in a public vehicle on a public road.

Yet I myself didn't like the taxi ride. People were uncomfortable with
Anna and me in the car. There were rules for how to act around veiled Muslim women, but the Arab men did not know how to act with us and with me
especially; I knew it was because I was unveiled and of a marriageable age.

They were respectful and courteous, but often didn't speak to us. Even the Arab women in the taxi said nothing, so I was happy when the Haqs agreed to let us ride with them.

Shamshad Haq was old enough to be wearing the chador, but in the car, she didn't keep her face veiled. Shamshad was quiet and reserved. Her father was a wealthy merchant, one in a dynasty of Indian merchants who had been traders in Aden for at least a century. Today it was not the chauffeur, but Faizan, at the wheel.

"Hi, Faizan, how come you are driving today?" Faizan was Shamshad's brother. He was very good looking, I thought, and very friendly.

"I have some business in Steamer Point, so I thought I would drive you girls to school." Faizan smiled. He was slim, of medium height with black slicked-back hair. As always, he was dressed impeccably, in creased slacks and a snow-white shirt. He wore a gold chain around his neck. He worked in his father's business. His smile always gave me goose bumps.

I knew Faizan's wife was a Jewish woman and I spent much time thinking about how that marriage came about. Usually the family picked the bride for the young man, but obviously Faizan had made his own choice. Had he met her in her parents' store? How had he convinced his family to let him marry a Jewish woman? How had his wife been allowed to marry a Muslim? Her name was Fatima, an Arabic name; obviously, she must have converted to Islam. She must have been very much in love with him to give up her freedom. I had briefly met her at the Haq house where the whole extended family lived together. Fatima was gorgeous and ethereal in a floating organza dress, high-heeled shoes and expensive jewelry, but now, as a Muslim, she had to wear the chador when she went out! I could not believe that anyone should choose to wear a chador.

For some reason my mother didn't think Fatima had entered this marriage of her own free will. But I wasn't sure my mother really knew. Sometimes my mother made up her mind about things and then that was the way things were. She also expressed fears that the Haq family would try to seduce me into marrying Baboo, Faizan's younger brother. I could only laugh at that.

"How can you think that, Mummy? I'm only fourteen."

"You never know. Fourteen is a marriageable age for Muslims."

"Mum, we aren't Muslims."

My mother was inscrutable.

"Well, of course we would never allow it, and on second thought we probably are too poor for them."

What was she trying to say? I thought. My mother sometimes said strange things; she couldn't possibly mean what she said.

I got to know Baboo on a picnic Anna and I went on with the Haqs to The Gardens. This was a beautiful estate in Sheikh Othman surrounded by tall walls, not far from Kintore and The Manse. The Gardens had tennis courts and swimming pools. Several Indian families gathered for the picnic. In the garden, no one was veiled and everyone had fun. Some played tennis, and all swam and clowned around in the pool: Faizan, Fatima, Shamshad, Baboo and many other young people. We had water fights, and I found Baboo very funny and entertaining. Before that, I had thought him unattractive and boring. I had such a great time that I wished I could get to know the Haqs better.

At school Anna, Shamshad, and I hurried off to our respective classes. I was now in the upper level, one of the oldest students in the school. Many of my Muslim classmates had left to marry, just as the Reverend Mother had predicted, but there were still two girls at my level; they were daughters of British Officers, part of the large British contingent in the Colony of Aden.

Servicemen were everywhere in the Colony, young men who brought England with them, but who never seemed to take any particular interest in the local population, and who saw no need to learn Arabic. Their only contact with the natives was with the "boys," the servants they encountered in the mess hall, and the merchants in town, all of whom had enough English to understand the needs of these young men. Their needs were various and sundry and what they had least of were young women their own age. There were only a few European girls, some of them daughters of commissioned officers, among them Gillian and Miranda, my schoolmates.

Miranda was a shy girl who lived with her parents at the Air Base at Khormaksar. Gillian, however, was older and more experienced. Gillian wore lipstick and make-up, went to adult parties, and drank gin-and-tonics, facts that fascinated and intrigued me, though at that age I harbored enough of my parents' puritanism to view Gillian's behavior as somewhat licentious. Gillian partied with the families of the high-ranking officers that lived around Telegraph Hill and danced at the top of the Crescent Hotel in Steamer Point, singing along with the Big Band music blaring from the gramophone. With envy, I begged Gillian for all the details. I wanted to know all about these men, dressed in white, long pants and dress shirts, colored bow-ties at their necks, the women in wide skirted organza or taffeta dresses, heels so high they were sure to twist their ankles if they became drunk.

"Drunk!" I said. "Have you ever been drunk?"

Gillian giggled.

"Yes, once...I had too many gin-and-tonics."

"Wasn't that awful?"

"Yes, it was bloody awful, I don't think I'll ever do that again."

"You know that is very offensive to Muslims."

"What is? Getting drunk?"

"That too. I meant drinking alcohol."

"Oh, really. Well, those parties are just for us. Muslims aren't invited."

I felt myself torn between condemnation and fascination. I dreamed of dancing with a young man, being held tightly by him, his one arm on my low back, while he whispered in my ear. I longed for this with a deep aching. But drinking! And all that went along with that, as my parents said. I myself didn't know what they meant, and I wasn't going to ask Gillian. But obviously it was nothing good.

We spent much time talking about young men. I found myself very attracted to a young serviceman I saw on Sundays at church, and with whom I exchanged notes and photos. Bryan's handwriting was beautiful, his rhetoric inflated, funny, and self-deprecating, but we didn't go on dates. My parents would never allow that; after all, I was only fourteen and he nineteen. Once, however, Anna and I were allowed to go to an evening meeting at the Anglican Church at Khormaksar and Bryan asked me to take a walk with him before my father came to pick up Anna and me. Anna, however, insisted on accompanying us and I lacked the cunning to find a plausible excuse to leave her behind. Thus, I lost my chance at my first kiss. For a long time I mourned that loss.

I was the only serious student at my class level. Gillian was passing time, and Miranda had no interest in continuing her education. I, however, loved learning and had set myself the goal of becoming a doctor, an ambitious goal, but since my first trip up-country with uncle Raymond this ambition had gradually taken hold of me. I wanted to become a medical missionary.

That day in school Mother Superior called me out of class and asked me to come to her office. I had not been in that office since the very first day when I had met the old nun. A new, much younger Mother Superior—an Italian—had been my teacher for the past year. I liked her very much, but I had no idea why she might want to talk to me. A few weeks before, she had separated us three girls because we talked too much—about boys—but I thought we had been exemplary in recent days.

After we sat down Mother Superior said:

"You are doing very well in school…" I accepted the compliment though I didn't think it quite true, "and I hardly have more to teach you…."

So, what was she going to tell me? That I couldn't go to school anymore. But I would miss Gillian and Miranda!

"…but I thought you might want to finish your education with us by taking the Senior Cambridge University Examination for Overseas Students. It is the highest examination we offer here in the Colony. It might be to your advantage to take it."

My first thought was that maybe I could then stay in school longer.

"We will help you prepare for it. I will give you some information to take home to your parents and they can come in and talk to me about it."

"So I can continue in school?"

"Oh, certainly."

My parents and I agreed with the Reverend Mother. I liked studying, but what was more, I wanted to stay in school so I could continue to be with the only peers I had. I finally had friends my own age again and I didn't want to be separated from them. So, we made the decision that I should take the exam.

When the day of the examination came, I did not feel well prepared. My father drove me to the new Government High School in Sheikh Othman and I entered the examination room with apprehension. I found that I was the only white, and the only young woman, out of twenty-four students sitting for the examination. I felt self-conscious and intimidated by having to take the exam in the company of all these young men, all of them older than me, Indians and Arabs who seemed much more confident than I was.

Afterwards I had no sense of how I had done and awaited the results with fatalism. I told myself that it was not important that I pass the exam, as I was not continuing my education in Britain!

Nonetheless, when I received a call from the Director of Education that I had passed, I was gratified.

The Abyss

The plane was full, all twenty passenger-seats taken. It was 1952 and my family and I were heading into the interior highlands of the British Protectorate for our yearly summer vacation. As the plane took off, I noticed a small Arab girl sitting next to Anna reaching out for Anna's hand.

"I've never been on a plane before," the child whispered. "I'm scared."

Anna, who feared nothing, reassuringly took the girl's hand and smiled back at me. The small B.O.A.C. plane tracked its way north across the desert. It was a clear day, but a uniform haze of sand and humidity obscured the ground. As the plane gained altitude and we came further north, the air became drier and we could now make out mountains below us.

The airport bus had come for us at four-thirty that morning, and we arrived at the airport in Khormaksar as the sun rose. Abdullah was with us; he wanted to see an airplane up close. As we waited in the airport restaurant, Abdullah spotted an Egyptian plane preparing to depart. With rising excitement, he noted that the passengers were going on the Hajj.

"I hope to do that one day," he said with great assertion. " That is the greatest thing a Muslim can do." Raising his hand and pretending to be holding rupee bills between his fingers he grinned: "When I get enough *filus* (money), I'll go."

My parents laughed at Abdullah's ambition, but I was sure they secretly hoped that if he ever got enough money he would spend it differently. The passengers appeared wealthy and I doubted Abdullah would ever be able to afford it. Yet I did not doubt his sincerity.

"Why do people go on the Hajj?"

"The prophet Muhammed—Peace be upon Him—said that every Muslim who could afford it should do the Hajj at least once in his life. The Hajj is a pilgrimage to Mecca—to the *Ka'bah*, which you must circumscribe seven times. See, I know these things."

"Oh, you're always a show-off," I laughed.

He wanted to come with us to Mukeiras.

"*As-Sitt* (the Lady-of-the-house) can't do without me. Who will go to the market to shop? Who will light the kerosene stove? Who will wash the dishes?" He looked at my mother pleadingly. "And you won't understand the dialect there. You need me to translate for you."

We all shook our heads. "No! Abdullah," my mother said, "we can manage. Besides, *as-Sahib* (the Master) understands the dialect."

"You just want to go on the plane!" I said.

"Yeah, I'd really like that."

Just then an imam on the tarmac intoned "*Allahu akbar, allahu akbar, allahu akbar*," and the Egyptian plane started moving away.

"God is great indeed," Abdullah said.

Thirty minutes later, we were in Mukeiras. There was no airport; the landing strip was just a grassy field. A group of local Arabs greeted the arriving passengers; an older man and a young boy came up to us. They were servants from the British Government Rest House coming to help us with the luggage. They loaded it into two wheelbarrows and brought it to the house, not two hundred yards away.

The buildings, of gray lava rocks and white mortar, surrounded a central courtyard, which we entered through a large gate. At the other end were a lounge and a dining room. Flanking the grassy courtyard on both sides were two bedroom suites. No one occupied the suites; my parents, Anna, and I were the only guests, but more were expected. The place was intimidating, large and empty, and situated far from any of the surrounding villages. We had been assigned rooms at either side of the courtyard and I at once was uncomfortable about sleeping so far from my parents. Afterwards, I thought I should have known how threatening this place would become to me.

Yet the surroundings drew me in. The Rest House sat on a little knoll. From the living room, we had a view of the bare mountains and of the green valleys that stretched along riverbeds. These valleys were filled with fruit orchards: peach, orange, lemon, fig, and quince, and with fields of millet and sorghum. On the bare mountains surrounding the house, little villages were strategically placed at points from where advancing enemies could be seen. We spent our days exploring the countryside. My father, Anna, and I—not my mother who feared walking here lest she should fall and break a bone— daily went for long hikes over the mountains and along the green valleys. On our way, we met weather-beaten old women, young wives, girls, and small boys carrying huge bundles of wood. They made long treks every day, scrounging for firewood. My father, Anna and I visited villages clinging to the mountainside where my father used his medical knowledge to treat the occasional patient with skin ulcers.

On our return, we all helped my mother prepare dinner. Later, when evening fell, we lit the kerosene lamps, curled up in comfortable chairs in the lounge and with my mother knitting and I embroidering, my father read to us. The living room enveloped us in warm light, but I was apprehensive. Nighttime was approaching and I feared going to sleep in my room. Most often, the pleasurable daytime activities kept my nighttime fear somewhat under cover. But when we retired to our suites at night, and when I went to bed under the comforting canopy of the mosquito net, I fought giving myself up to sleep. I was assailed by panic and dread. I lay stiff and petrified in bed, afraid of falling asleep. Falling asleep meant losing control of my mind and there was no way of knowing what tricks it might play on me.

One day when we had followed a green valley for many kilometers it seemed, we all of a sudden found ourselves standing at the edge of a canyon about a thousand feet deep. It was a spectacular view; the river below was just a ribbon winding through the green valley, and in the distance were hazy, blue mountains. The three of us were amazed and overwhelmed. We knew nothing of this chasm. We carefully moved closer to the edge, apprehensive and afraid of plunging over the side to our deaths in the river far below. Later this abyss for me would come to symbolize the precipice I felt myself hurtling towards while in Mukeiras.

There was enough to scare me there: the scorpion in the bathtub and people shooting off their guns at the door. The latter at first disturbed us all until we realized that this was how the local people announced themselves.

Yet those events did not bring on the dread; I was not afraid of reality. My fear was of nothing real or tangible, but of something within me I couldn't define, and in the twilight zone between wakefulness and sleep that fear grew to irrational proportions.

When I got into bed one night I thought, maybe if I stayed alert, this fear would not swallow me up and destroy me. If I stayed alert, maybe I could keep my mind under control.

I sat up in bed, my heart pounding, my breathing rapid. I could not let myself go to sleep; if I did, my mind would have free reign. I considered going to my parents, but their room seemed immeasurably far away, across the rain-soaked courtyard.

Eventually however—Anna had called across the courtyard—my father came to our room and made me settle down. He talked to me in a calming voice as he sat by my bedside.

"I'll stay with you till you go to sleep," he said.

I relaxed. I was tired. I started dropping off to sleep, but again I jerked awake. I realized that once I was asleep my father would leave. I would be alone; dread would again overwhelm me.

I begged my father to stay. He agreed and took Anna to my parents' room. He then came back to sleep in Anna's bed, at my side, but the dread never completely left me.

I remembered having experienced this unease about nighttime the last summer I stayed with my godparents at the vicarage in Denmark. I slept in my tiny room with the paying guest next door. During the many summers I spent there, I had always liked the little room until the summer I first experienced severe homesickness. Like a poison, it invaded my whole being. Nothing was enjoyable anymore. The activities with my godparents' boys, activities that in other years had seemed so exciting—playing hide-and-seek in the oat fields, climbing the trees, biking to nearby villages, riding the horses—were no longer fun.

And always there was this dread of nighttime when I was alone in my tiny room, the room I had treasured so much before. My godmother tucked me in, then left me, and I lay in dread waiting for the paying guest, a kindly woman, to come to the adjoining room. When she came, the light in her room, her activity, her reassuring conversation calmed me. But the home-sickness wouldn't leave and finally the only solution had been to go home, which I did that year, with many regrets.

At Mukeiras heavy rains at night soaked the world around us, turning the valleys vividly green. The rain pelted against the ground in the courtyard, pock-marking it. The landing strip became soft and inaccessible and no other visitors came. We were alone and isolated from the world. Yet our days were as before. We continued our walks and visits to the villages during the day, and at night my father read. He was now reading Dickens's *David Copperfield,* and, when the rains kept us in Mukeiras two weeks past our departure date; when day after day the plane was canceled; when we were contemplating departing over the steep pass, my mother on a donkey, and realized the impossibility and hilarity of that; and when we thought we were trapped forever in those mountains, we jokingly pronounced with the ever optimistic Mr. Wilkins Micawber: "Something will turn up!"

But as ten o'clock came closer, fear gripped me. By bedtime, the fear had escalated into full-blown panic and the whole confusing circus started all over again.

And night after night, the rains continued to fall.

I wrote about our daily experiences in my diary. Keeping my mind occupied I spent hours writing while a little worm ate away at my heart:

Sunday our cook, Qassim, invited Anna and me to his house in Salool for the sacrificial slaughtering for the Feast of the Lamb. We went with him to his house in the village...From his courtyard the lamb was led up the outside stairs to the roof. We followed. Here the sacrificial ceremony took place. A village elder whose name was Abdu Nabi (servant of the Prophet) per-formed the ritual. A basin of lightly salted water was set before the sheep. Abdu Nabi intoned *Allahu akbar* three times. The lamb, uncomprehending, drank the water. Abdu Nabi immersed its feet, one by one, in the basin; with each dipping, he again chanted *Allahu akbar* three times. One of the men took the sheep by its legs and laid it on its side. Abdu Nabi brought out a sharp knife, slashed its throat, dragged it to the edge of the roof, and let the blood, gushing from its neck, run down the outside wall of the house. When all the blood was drained, Abdu Nabi took the sheep down into the courtyard, tied its hind legs with a rope, hung it from a nail, and proceeded to skin it.

As I read the diary fifty years later, I become aware that my fifteen-year-old self's meticulous entry about the ceremony is devoid of any emotion. I wrote neither about my feelings regarding the sacrificial ceremony, nor about my fears and nighttime dread. Yet I, even at my present age, can again almost sense the dread I felt as a fifteen-year-old. I wonder if for my young self to acknowledge my despair in writing had meant admitting its reality. Was I attempting to stay in control in order to preserve my integrity as a person? Sometimes I find it hard to understand my younger self, yet I know how being out of control can produce chaos and cause a sense of failure. One thing neither the young nor the mature I had ever wanted was to be a failure. By not writing about it, might I have been pretending to myself that I was able to control my fear, thus allowing myself to believe it never occurred?

And the rains did not let up. The small streams swelled and turned into rivers rushing through the valleys in the early morning only to peter out later in the day when the hot sun parched the ground. The rain was a balm that should have soothed me as I listened to it drumming on the roof at night; instead I found it somber and threatening. Meanwhile, I wrote:

Qassim invited us into his living room where he served us *khubz-at-tawwa*, a flat oven-baked bread, hardboiled eggs, and sweet tea with ginger. Though not hungry—we had just had breakfast—we accepted. It would have been an affront to refuse it.

We then went out into the courtyard to see Abdu Nabi butchering the lamb according to ancient laws. A fourteen-year-old niece of Qassim,

Haleema, watching with us, left abruptly when Abdu Nabi Jr. arrived; she was his betrothed. Though she wore no veil and could be seen by the other men of the village, the one she was to marry could not see her.

We left to visit our "boy," Mohammed Hanëish's, house. A young man there gave us four eggs and two cups of fresh milk. Mohammed Hanëish brought us fried liver from the newly slaughtered lamb; we ate it and found it delicious.

Finally, we visited the house of two other friends of Qassim's. Their wives wanted to paint our faces, so we could be as beautiful as they were. They painted a red streak along the hairline, ocher paint was spread lightly over our foreheads and down onto the cheeks. The women created discrete circular spots of brighter ocher in the middle of our foreheads and temples and at last put mascara on our eyes. They thought we were very beautiful. They had now appropriately decorated us for the dance celebration that was to take place. They invited us to participate.

The women danced in pairs, one of them beating a drum. Then they lined up in two rows dancing back and forth, toward and away from each other, all the while beating the drums and singing songs whose words we did not understand. We tried to follow their lead. They smiled and laughed, at us and with us. We moved back and forth like the women, toward each other, away from each other; but we felt out of place in our short sundresses and with our strangely painted faces. These women and girls were so beautiful; they were so delicate and lithe. They moved to the rhythms with such assurance. Their long, beautiful dresses swooped the ground, bright georgette scarves circled their hair, and intricate patterns in reddish-brown henna covered their hands and feet.

I was the age of the young girl who was soon to marry her betrothed and who was happy doing what her family expected of her. My life was vastly different, but I too knew my parents' expectations and I was eager to fulfill them. Ever since I first expressed a desire to become a doctor, my parents had encouraged me. I knew they fully expected me to achieve my goals.

But during my time in Mukeiras—as a young fifteen-year-old—I felt so alone that I doubted I could ever grow up to become an independent person let alone a doctor. Would I always feel this way? Nobody seemed capable of helping me. Though my parents tried, they could not reach into my soul and turn off whatever created this chaos.

It stopped raining, and we knew that "something would turn up" soon. Within the week, when the ground was dry, the plane would be here.

Saturday Dad, Anna, and I made a visit to Aryoob, the main town, four miles away. There were no roads and no cars. We followed one of the ancient paths that have connected the villages since time immemorial, across a mountain from which we saw the town. On the mountain we met Naib as-Sultan Abdullah bin Ahmed, the Sultan's deputy (Naib), and his retinue. He was a young man of about thirty, a cousin of the Sultan of Zara. He was friendly and invited us to his house for tea.

We followed the company to his "palace," a four-storied building. Though beautifully decorated and large compared to the one-storied mud houses surrounding it, it bore little resemblance to a European's concept of a palace. He invited us into his gardens that contained beautiful fruit trees and vegetable plots. He gave us cabbage and quinces.

We entered the "palace" and went up the uneven stone steps to a room at the top that had a bed for a sofa, covered with intricately patterned rugs. On the floor, along the walls, were brightly colored velour cushions; in the middle of the room was a large oriental carpet. All the shutters were closed, but sunlight filtered through the cracks and light fell on the room from an electric bulb hanging from the ceiling. Electricity was provided from a generator. After removing our shoes, we were invited to sit down and were given sweet tea with ginger and some biscuits.

This was where the qat sessions took place, but we were neither offered qat nor invited to smoke the beautifully decorated brass water pipes that sat in the middle of the carpet. We conversed politely with the Deputy-Sultan and his male family. The Naib was a very kind man, but had difficulty understanding us. He apparently was very good to the people and was well liked. As we took leave, we invited him to visit us at the Rest House....

The Naib made a return visit the next day, arriving on a gray horse. With him was the brother of the Sultan of Zara, Ga'abel Ahmed bin Hussein, on a fiery black Arabian. He is eighteen and is the most beautiful young man I have ever seen. His black hair was oiled, shoulder length and curly. His handsome face with the prominent cheekbones was smiling; his headscarf, the *mushadda*, wound around the forehead, was of cashmere. His shirt and futa were of beautiful silk cloth, his sandals of decorated leather. At his waist, a *gambiyya*, the curved double-edged short sword, was couched in a holster decorated with gold and precious stones. He had the proud, confident bearing characteristic of his people. I couldn't help falling in love with him. They stayed for a short while, had tea, praised my mother's cake, and rode off in a canter.

The grass strip was now dry enough for the plane to land and to our relief we were able to return to Aden.

Ga'abel appeared in Crater shortly after. Anna and I met him on our evening walks to the beach. We conversed politely. He said he would soon be leaving for England. Every time I met him, my heart skipped a beat. I dreamt about him. I wanted to know more about him; I wanted to know what his life was like, what his plans and dreams were. But he was quiet, and I found it difficult to understand his dialect. Besides, an entourage of men always surrounded him; a fact that made prolonged conversations difficult. And then, he was gone. I did not see him again.

This young man fascinated me, but a cultural and religious chiasm separated us. He was friendly and polite, and despite yearning for love, I knew this was forbidden territory.

And my nighttime fears did not end with our vacation. Many were the nights when I could not, or would not, sleep, and my father would calm me. Was this the precursor of the depressions that would affect me later on?

Worries and Disappointment

Dr. Alan Fawdry often took my mother to the General Hospital to visit Mrs. Gardner, an English woman who suffered from acute poliomyelitis and was in an iron lung. Alan was the government physician who lived with us at Hebron while his family was in England. My mother loved taking care of single, incompetent men and took him in like a stray cat. Alan was tall and scrawny, his unkempt hair often hung in his eyes. He lived in the conference room and shared Abdullah's bathroom.

My mother told us about her visits to Mrs. Gardner. Often she heard the motor of the iron lung as soon as she stepped into the hospital corridor. Once in the room all she could see was Mrs. Gardner's head sticking out of the respirator. Mrs. Gardner couldn't move, but could see my mother in a mirror that had been rigged up for her. She had been there for quite some time already. She came down with polio just before the Red Cross ship arrived in the harbor with the polio vaccinations. My parents, Anna and I along with the entire population of Aden received our vaccinations from the Red Cross, but by then it was too late for Mrs. Gardner.

My mother wondered how she could stand it, being locked up in a box as she was, with only her head sticking out. And how she must worry that the generator would not come on during power outages of which there were many. My mother knew that someone was with Mrs. Gardner almost all the time, but what if the power outage happened at the exact moment no one was there. My mother went to Mrs. Gardner's bedside once a week to read for her as it was hard for Mrs. Gardner to pass the time. She really wished she was back in England, but it was too risky to move her. What if something failed on the way?

There had been a polio epidemic and many people had become sick, but Mrs. Gardner's was the worst British case. She had been put in the only iron lung available in the colony; surely anyone diagnosed later and who couldn't breathe either, must have died. We assumed that after the vaccinations there would be no more cases and we could relax.

At home I enjoyed playing on the piano Dr. Fawdry had brought with him when he moved in. I had long wanted a piano, but now I wished I had piano music as well. All I had to play from were hymnals; I wanted to work on piano pieces. We had previously had a harmonium in the house. I had played on it, but did not like it. It was so limiting. I fervently wished I could have continued my piano lessons; I had always been fond of practicing, and had spent hours at the piano in Aarhus. But not only were there no teachers, there was also no piano music to be had.

I think my mother found it difficult having teen-age children in general, and in Aden especially. My father seemed to handle us better, and he certainly now showed more concern for me than my mother did. Some time after the polio epidemic my mother was not doing well. Often she was in bed for days with curtains drawn. Did she have headaches, or was she depressed? We were not told what ailed her. For some time she seemed unable to participate in anything.

But our parents did worry about us and what we might be exposed to. The following probably had an impact on their increasing concerns. Just before summer vacation, my father had sent Abdullah's cousin packing. My parents had allowed Abdullah to take in the cousin, as he had nowhere to stay. One day my father had found him masturbating on my bed. My father had become livid with anger and had thrown him out. My parents must have been happy that we were at school.

On the other hand they considered the young American missionary couple next-door a positive influence. Anna and I often went there to entertain their young children. The Americans also had meetings for young people where many of the RAF men showed up and we loved being at those meetings. But our parents were careful that we were well supervised even around those young men.

Around this time something happened for my parents that turned a positive development in their evangelizing efforts into a disappointment. A baptism and marriage of a young Arab couple the year before at the Scottish Mission was becoming a nightmare. Our parents had had so many hopes for them.

In 1946 the young man, Mustafa, had come to my father saying he wanted to become a Christian. He had led an unsettled life. His father was a Yemeni living in self-imposed exile in Ethiopia, his mother French, but he had spent his teen-age years with an uncle in Eritrea and there he had been exposed to missionaries. For some reason he had come to Aden. He told my father he had heard so much about Christ and wanted to follow his teachings.

My father had prepared him for baptism over a long period and the Scottish mission had given him a job, as he had no way of supporting himself. Yet there had been some problems with him and they had been reluctant to baptize him. He had been involved with prostitutes and had not minded his job, and so they had had to discipline him. He had been very contrite, however, and had promised to do better, and they had become convinced that he was sincere and that he wanted to become a Christian.

He desired to have a Christian wife. Shafiqa, a young woman that had attended the Danish Mission Girls' School, appeared a good match. Her father had died when she was in her early teens and her mother had married her off when she was fourteen; the mother was destitute and had many younger children to support. Shafiqa had an unhappy marriage, had born the man two children, one of whom died. And then her husband, who had been married before, took back his former wife and discarded Shafiqa. Thereafter she unsuccessfully tried to support herself and her little boy by sewing for people. She became very malnourished, and finally she had no one to turn to for help but the Mission. The missionaries thought the two young people could be a very good support for each other. The young couple met and agreed.

So finally, after prolonged preparations they had been baptized and married a few weeks later in the chapel of the Scottish Mission.

Things had gone well for many months; the Mission had found them a house and Mustafa had his job back at the Mission Hospital. And then—as my father said—the devil had entered their house in the form of Shafiqa's blind brother, a musician who worked for the prostitutes. Things had gone rapidly downhill, my parents weren't quite sure why, but the brother must have been a bad influence. Mustafa now often beat up Shafiqa, and his job performance became abysmal. He was finally fired. The couple's behavior in general was unacceptable to the missionaries. My father had worked hard to prepare them for baptism, and the missionaries had expected, or at least hoped, they would have been better Christian examples, but they had relapsed so easily into their former ways, even though the missionaries had tried hard to support them both spiritually and materially. Now that Mustafa was out of a job, my parents feared he could not resist the pressure to revert to Islam.

They felt frustrated. As my father wrote in one of the Mission's magazines: Had they not done their job right? Were they themselves poor examples of God's love? Had they not witnessed to the Glory of God and Christ? They prayed to God to forgive them their shortcomings and asked Him to continue to inspire in them faith and perseverance, and to keep Mustafa and Shafiqa as witnesses for Him.

Once again they realized how exceedingly difficult it was being a Christian, especially a converted Christian, in a Muslim country. As elsewhere in the world, the Gospel often attracted the disenfranchised in society, people who had little to lose by becoming Christians and much to gain. Unfortunately some of them were also often easily swayed and succumbed readily to pressures to denounce their newfound religion.

Just a Girl

With no school to attend I moped through December. I had sat for the Senior Cambridge University Examination in November of 1952 and had not gone back to school after that. The examination was the highest offered in the colony, and for further schooling one must go to India or England, neither a choice for me. Yet I had to stay in Aden until my family's return to Denmark in July of 1953.

I did not enjoy being home every day, where only Abdullah's presence cheered me. I made myself useful, helping my mother prepare for Christmas. We baked *vanillekranse* and *brune kager*, and other Danish cookies. I helped decorate the house and the small artificial tree, hanging the bright heart-shaped baskets that my siblings and I had cut out of glossy paper and braided back home, their colors red and green, and blue and yellow. I felt melancholy as I spread the tinsel across the branches. Though bored in my present situation, I now did not want to leave Aden. I loved it here, I loved the Arabs, I loved the exoticness, I loved the climate, and I dreaded the next transition. Yet I felt caged like an animal because our parents allowed us no freedoms. I went with my parents to church, to prayer meetings, and on picnics. This, my only enjoyment brought me out among people, kind and loving people who were like family in the minority community. Nevertheless, I longed to escape, I felt completely pent up. The constant presence of my parents implied constant supervision. The only time I was away from them was when Anna and I went for our evening walks—out of their sight.

My father was not happy that I was idle and encouraged me to find work. Fortunately, through my father's connection—Mr. Gunn at the Secretariat—there suddenly appeared a typist's job for which I could apply. I had been working on my typing skills since finishing school, but had never thought myself eligible for a job.

"I am so glad you will consider working for us here."

Mr. Murshid, the Head Clerk at the Secretariat, a small obsequious man, an Arab or an Indian, I did not know, welcomed me effusively when I came for an interview.

"I think you may like it here."

I wasn't so sure. I found everything rather intimidating.

"Oh, and I saw you passed the Senior Cambridge Overseas Examination. How wonderful. Only five passed. Aren't you rather young to have taken that exam?"

I didn't like being reminded of my young age, fifteen, especially now that I was hoping to get a job. I smiled self-consciously.

"Oh, yes, you should really be very pleased with yourself."

I felt a need to be honest.

"Mr. Murshid, I didn't do that well…I only achieved Grade 3…."

"Oh, but that is excellent, that is just excellent. So many try to take it and fail. No, no, you should be proud. And now you would like to become one of our typists?"

"Yes, I'd rather like that. I have been studying typing…"

"Yes, yes, that's what I understand. How many words can you type per minute?"

"Oh, I know I don't type nearly fast enough yet, but I am sure I'll get the hang of it."

"Well, not to worry, not to worry. You will do very well."

Before I knew it, Mr. Murshid hired me. He asked me to come back the next day to start. I quickly mentioned that I wasn't very good at stenography. I thought it better he be informed about that right away. Again, he told me not to worry.

I walked home elated. I had an actual job and would be going to work every day. I thought of all the money I could save up to spend when I went back to Europe in six months! My own money! On the other hand, I was also terrified. I wondered if I could live up to the expectations, although Mr. Murshid hadn't made it at all clear what his expectations were. I hoped my typing would improve rapidly.

Things had happened too quickly, I thought. One day I was in school, the next day I was a workingwoman. I worried I would be the only white at that level at the Secretariat, the only woman. I felt strange using that word for myself, a woman. I was really just a girl.

When I arrived for work the next day, Mr. Murshid showed me to the typists' room where I would be working. He introduced me to the only other typist there, Sayyed Anwar, an Indian who was in his late twenties or early thirties. Without a smile, he gave me a limp hand.

"Hello!" He looked at me briefly, his eyes expressing no curiosity.

"Hello," I murmured, "I'm so pleased to meet you…"

Turning away, Sayyed Anwar sat down at his desk, crushed his cigarette in the ashtray, and started typing. My heart sank a little But before his un-friendliness overwhelmed me, Mr. Murshid was talking away.

"Here is your desk, here the stationary. Why don't you sit down and become familiar with the typewriter. When you are done, come back to my desk and I will find you something to do. We'll be sure to keep you busy."

His solicitousness and friendliness made me feel a little better. I sat down, and quietly I explored my desk. The proximity of the silent Sayyed Anwar made me uneasy and I was mortified when I realized how fast he typed. I would never be able to type that fast!

Sayyed Anwar paid me no attention and I could think of nothing to say that would break the silence between us. I looked at him askance. He was good-looking, dressed in a crisp, snow-white shirt, open at the neck, with the sleeves turned up almost to the elbows; oiled black hair was combed away from the forehead, fingers were slim and long.

I was about to return to Mr. Murshid when to my dismay, I realized I didn't know my way back. Timidly I asked Sayyed Anwar. Typing away, he barely raised his head.

"Across the skywalk and through the junior clerks' room. You will find him at the other end."

"Thank you…" I edged out the door.

I hurried across the skywalk and into the clerks' cavernous room. Wide beams supported the high vault where skylights admitted a diffuse light. The sun never touched the desks below.

As I walked through the room, I felt the eyes of every clerk boring into me. I could not believe I hadn't noticed that when I came through with Mr. Murshid. I hardly knew what to do with myself. I just wanted to disappear. When I briefly raised my eyes to meet their gaze, they all looked down. I felt out of place and very conspicuous. With slumping shoulders, as if to deny my breasts, I looked straight ahead and forged my way between their desks. Finally, at the end of the room, I saw Mr. Murshid's smiling face, my safe haven, and I hurried toward him.

I spent my days writing letters Mr. Murshid dictated to me. Never learning stenography well enough, I took them down in longhand at his desk. The letters were mostly standard responses to inquiries dealing with the most mundane things: building permits, permits for storefronts…it seemed permission was needed for almost anything one could venture to do in the Colony.

I established a working relationship of sorts with Sayyed Anwar, asking him questions when I was in doubt, or when I needed something. His answers were economical, measured, and civil.

"May I borrow your white-out, please?" I asked.

"I'm so sorry. I have only one bottle. May I suggest you ask Mr. Murshid."

Folding letters and stuffing envelopes was an art of which he was the master. As I folded my first letter, Sayyed Anwar stopped me imperiously.

"That will never do!"

Without saying another word, he took the letter from me; meticulously he showed me how to fold it and then how to stuff it into the khaki-colored envelope in whose upper left corner were the words "On His Majesty's Service." King George was dead. The young Queen Elizabeth would be crowned in 1953, and before my job at the Secretariat was over all envelopes would have "On Her Majesty's Service" in the upper left corner.

Sometimes there was no conversation between Sayyed Anwar and me for days. We sat all day in total silence. I could not figure out Sayyed Anwar. I realized he wasn't mean-spirited; he was merely completely indifferent to me. It puzzled me. Was it impossible to be courteous? I thought. Why wouldn't he talk? Or was it so difficult to smile, be pleasant, or just a little friendly?

Sayyed Anwar handled the most important letters and by far the majority of the typing. Chain-smoking, he hammered away at the keys as one completed letter after another piled up on his desk. After having been at the Secretariat for a few weeks, I realized that the efficient Sayyed Anwar was fully capable of handling all the typing for Mr. Murshid. Had I been a little more perceptive I might have wondered if my job was created for me, but that thought did not cross my mind.

Periodically Sayyed Anwar left the room to have sweet Arabic tea outside the building and to talk to other clerks and I was persuaded that he *could* talk. Just not to me. At other times, he left to go to the nearby mosque to pray. I quietly enjoyed those times when I had the office to myself, and while Mr. Anwar was out I sneaked looks at his letters to see how he lined things up on the page; eventually I got the knack of it and typed to Mr. Murshid's satisfaction.

Several times a day, I made my way through the gloomy, cavernous room where junior Indian and Arab clerks worked. All appeared to be working intensely. Interminably a clerk pored over a stack of papers, then, when done he studiously gathered up the pile, and moving carefully between desks he self-importantly presented them to another clerk, then wended his way back to his own chair, sat down and scrutinized another pile. It was like a solemn, slowly orchestrated dance, a game of never-ending musical papers. Some piles were never moved. They accumulated under layers of dust and soon no one knew what they were about. They remained stacked where they were. "His Majesty's" papers were sacred. Occasionally papers reached their final destination, Mr. Murshid's desk, where he made a decision and dictated a letter to Sayyed Anwar or me.

One day a young, single English woman, Miss May, came to work with Sayyed Anwar and me at the Secretariat. She had come out to Aden because the man she hoped to marry was stationed there. Miss May was experienced.

She had been a typist for two years back in England. Assessing the situation in the typists' room, a staff of only two, a fifteen-year-old white girl and a thirty-year-old Indian man, she quickly concluded that she was invaluable. The addition of Miss May crowded the small room. Sayyed Anwar became even more uncommunicative, he barely deigned to bestow a look at Miss May when he arrived for work, let alone say good morning. Yet, Miss May was friendly and vivacious, maybe a little flighty. There was always so much outside her job that craved her attention, and it was important that she took part in the British social scene.

It quickly became apparent, however, that Miss May was not nearly as proficient as Sayyed Anwar. He still did the bulk of the work, piling up letter after letter in his out-basket. Quietly he worked away while Miss May was busy filing her nails or reapplying lipstick. I became uneasy as the level of Sayyed Anwar's irritability rose.

Finally, Miss May received her first paycheck. She complained bitterly to me that she would never be able to make ends meet on that salary. Yes, she knew she made more than Sayyed Anwar, but her expenses were so much greater.

"You are alone," I said, " Sayyed Anwar has a wife and children."

"Yes, but still…" her haughtiness cut through the air, "…I am white."

Thus, I spent my last months in Aden, working and yearning for another life. I felt at lose ends after finishing school and was uncertain about my future in Denmark. I was a dutiful child who throughout my childhood had acquiesced and continued to do so until I left my parents' home a year later. During my childhood in Aarhus I remember little of any relationship to God, but while in Aden I burned with faith, and shared my parents' mission. I bore it as a badge of honor when Arabs shouted after my sister and me in the streets: "*Benat el-mughawwi*," they are the daughters of the one who leads us astray from our religion. I also faithfully assisted my parents in their evangelizing church service every Sunday at Beit-ash-sharif by playing the harmonium in accompaniment of Arabic hymns. I had been cast in the role of the dutiful daughter, a role I would never entirely shed.

On June 23, 1953, we left Aden on one of the P&O liners. Shortly before on June 2, 1953, Queen Elizabeth the Second was crowned and huge parades and fireworks had taken place in Aden. This was like a last hurrah on the Eve of the Collapse of the British Empire. Fourteen years later Aden gained independence.

Though unexcited about my return to Denmark, I became pragmatic. A chapter in my life had ended, a chapter that would shape my life in ways I could not have anticipated; but I resolved to avoid looking back and to embrace the future whatever it would bring—happiness and prosperity, challenges, and sadness.

Kintore.

Scottish Mission Hospital, Sheikh Othman

The author's father (far left) poses with members of the medical staff and daughters,
on and next to a Land-Rover in Gi'ar, Aden Protectorate, 1951
(on the bumper: Ibrahim Bain, the author's sister Anna, and the author).

Anna, the author, a member of the medical staff, and a soldier in Mudia,
Aden Protectorate, 1951.

Shepherd boy with flute and Anna, Mudia, Aden Protectorate, 1951.

The author's family's house (Hebron) in Crater in the British Crown Colony of Aden, 1952.

Abdullah, the author's family's "boy," picture taken in 1955.

Crater and the two-thousand-year-old water tanks.

Villager and child in Mukeiras, 1952.

The author (left) and her sister Anna on the fortifications, in the British Crown Colony of Aden, 1953.

The author and her husband Johannes ("Hans") on their wedding day, 1959.

Looking Back

(1981)

Two Generations

Dad, I'll clean up."

I am in my parents' kitchen, a long, narrow room with a small refrigerator on one side, a stove, and a counter on the other, and by the window a sink. It faces north, yet it is light and airy; the cabinets are painted white. But the walls are flaking and the lamp over the stove is yellow from cooking fumes. Fifteen years ago, thinking ahead to when they could no longer take care of themselves, my parents chose this one bedroom flat in an apartment building connected to a nursing home.

My eighty-four year old father is standing in the doorway. His smile is uneasy at my intrusion into his domain.

"No, you are a visitor. I'll clean up. You have come all the way from America to visit us, not to do dishes."

"No, Dad. I am tired of sitting. Let me do it, please."

It is 1981 and I am forty-four years old.

I had left Minnesota the day before, arriving in Copenhagen early in the morning, and had taken a commuter plane to Aarhus. A hired car took me the twenty-five miles into town to my parents' place. I am aware that my parents think I waste money—I *could* have taken the Airport Bus—but they don't say anything.

They had met me at the door, my father with tears in his eyes. His over-emotional response was a little unsettling; on the other hand, I knew he had become more labile with age. They hugged me. I don't know when this hugging started, we are not a family given to physical demonstrations of love; maybe Anna and I—the two daughters living in the U.S.—had Americanized them in this.

The years did not appear to have affected my father. Only recently had his fringe of hair gone gray. Age spots dotted his baldpate; the tip of his nose and one ear bore evidence of excised basal cell carcinomas: battle scars from his life in the tropics. He tended to lean forward a bit, but otherwise had not changed. Mum on the other hand was now using canes to get around and Dad did most of the housework. Furrowed wrinkles coursed her cheeks. She wore her thin gray hair pulled back in a bun, covered with a hairnet; the way she had always kept it. It had made her look old even when I was a child.

I look around the small kitchen. Errant knives have scarred the worn linoleum on the counter top and black mold congregates around the faucets. Innumerable pints of tea consumed have stained the insides of the cups I am about to wash.

I feel claustrophobic in the small apartment. Ten days! I'll go crazy before it is time to go home again.

The kitchen smells stale. I throw open the window. The day is mild, spring comes early in Denmark, and already the geraniums on the balconies across the street are flowering. My eyes fall on the bike-stand by the entrance, which is overflowing with well-worn, rusty bikes. My father's bike is no longer there. Until recently, he had biked to the store daily, carrying home the groceries in a bag hanging from the handlebars, but he has finally realized walking is safer.

My parents don't have a dishwasher; they wash their dishes by hand. Mostly what it amounts to is rinsing them under hot water. They seem to think they don't get anything dirty. I usually don't enter their kitchen; they want to treat me as a visitor and I indulge them. But today, still unsettled, it bothers me to have to drink out of a stained cup. Before coming, I had been very busy at home and I don't want to put brakes on my efficiency. I want to put one job behind me so I can get on with the next. The sink with food remnants dotting its sides, its bottom stained dark, challenges me. I reach for the Ajax under the sink. A smell of mildew hits me. How can they stand it? I vigorously scrub the sink until my frustration drains out of me, and the stainless steel rewards me with a gleaming shiny surface. I pull all the cups out of the cupboard and scrub them clean, dry them and put them back. I reach for the glass coffee pot, the insides of which is coated in oily residue. As my hand scrubs it, the pot breaks in my hand.

"What's taking so long?"

My father is at the door. He sees the broken coffee pot; I smile apologetically.

"I scrubbed it. It broke. I'll get another one later. I'll just wash the floor and then I'm done."

I pretend not to see the hurt look on my father's face.

"Well, I suppose I should thank you for doing this, but…do you really think we are such pigs?" His smile is gentle and timid. I feel chastised.

"I know you have been doing this for years, Dad. But maybe you can't see that the cups aren't clean. Maybe your eyes aren't that good any longer…"

Somehow, I know I have said the wrong thing. He does not want my criticism, nor does he want to hear about his failings, and I think: Who am I to come flying in from America turning their world upside down? They are doing fine, taking care of themselves, and of each other. I feel like an intruder.

This visit is like a tour of duty where I have to take myself totally out of the picture. I can forget about being efficient and solving problems. As far as they are concerned, they have no problems. They feel competent and able to handle their day-to-day situation. They are coping well. I must give myself totally over to their way of living while I am here, I think.

"Let me help you take your stuff to your room," my father says. He carries my suitcase as I follow him through the basement, and up the stairs of the nursing home.

"I can carry that, Dad."

"So can I," he says smilingly, pushing demonstratively ahead of me. I can barely keep up.

My room is on the first floor of the nursing home. We walk through the institutional kitchen and down a hallway at the far end of the building. It feels like coming home; I have stayed here so often over the years. The room has white unadorned walls, two twin beds, a table and a chair, a mirror; the bathroom is down the hall. I like the simplicity of it.

My father goes back to the apartment for his nap. I unpack and lie down on one of the beds.

So here I am again. Every year I make this pilgrimage home. In late winter or spring I take ten days off from my practice. Before leaving I do anticipatory catch- up, put in long hours at work, take extra call, clear my desk of paperwork, and this year, on my way out of town, I stopped to testify in a court case. I was exhausted when I finally sat on the plane, my mind still reeling with the intensity of my court appearance. I felt I had been unnecessarily tough and uncompromising in my opinions. I tried unsuccessfully to put it behind me and was unable to sleep on the plane. I am even more exhausted now. I know that this will not be a vacation. It's a sort of penance I pay for having left Denmark, for not being there for my parents in their old age. But now at least, I can catch up on my sleep; there is no phone in my room.

It is very quiet in this part of the nursing home; it is far enough from the highway that I don't hear the traffic. The only noises that reach me are bewildered residents on the floor above crying out in the middle of the night, and early morning clanging of pots and pans from the nearby kitchen.

I try to relax while I think back on the weeks preceding my departure. About a month ago, I was diagnosed with a malignant melanoma and had it removed. I believe it has been taken care of, yet doubts linger, and I still await a pathology review. Yet I am optimistic and try not to dwell on the negative.

I fall into a dead sleep.

Later in the afternoon I have coffee with my parents. I sit on the couch they have had for fifty-two years. They had it re-upholstered a long time ago, in garish bright blue and light gray; it is now worn again.

"We don't want to spend money on new furniture or having this set upholstered again; it will last us our time out," they say. They have said this for the last twenty years. My mother sits in a chair, knitting. Her vision is deteriorating as cataracts cloud her eyes, and sometimes she drops a stitch without realizing it.

"Mum, when are you going to have surgery on your eyes?"

"I am not going to have anything done."

"Why? It is a very small operation."

"I don't want anyone to touch my eyes," Mum's voice is dangerously stubborn. We have had this discussion before. Mum has made up her mind and nothing can change it. It is as if she already is preparing for death. What's the point of having her eyes fixed? I find it unfair of her to put this extra burden on Dad. Mum already has some early symptoms of Alzheimer's disease. She forgets, she gets angry, and lashes out at my father for no seeming reason, something not in character for her. Maybe the Alzheimer's would not progress so rapidly, if Mum could see and if she continued to have outside stimulation.

"So you thought you would give the kitchen a good cleaning?" my mother says accusingly.

I shrug my shoulders.

"I like to clean, it relaxes me. Why don't you just let me do it?"

"No, no, Dad can do it, he is more mobile and sees better than I. We know how hard you work at home. We want you to take it easy while you are here."

They are unusually solicitous to me. I sigh. They want to turn back the clock, to reclaim the young dutiful daughter I once was, and they want me to sit at their feet and listen.

My father tells me about the book they are reading, what has happened in it so far, and asks if I would like to listen.

"Sure!" I say.

I take out the cross-stitch I bought when I was last in Aarhus and for which I had no time at home. I relax and let my father's voice wash over me. This is the way it always was. These were our best times together: my father reading, Mum doing needlework, and Anna and I listening. As often was the case, the book my father has now chosen is a moral story, a book that fails to hold my interest. Yet I finally feel curiously free of worry; my stressful job as a physician, the recently discovered melanoma, my husband, my teen-aged children belong in a different world.

Here, I am my parents' child.

I strain my eyes to see the cross-stitch. The light is poor in this corner of my parents' living room. I enjoy the orderliness of cross-stitching, the exactness required. If I miscount a thread, the whole design will be off; there is no room for error.

Throughout my father's reading my mother chimes in with little commentaries, as if she were a member of a black, southern congregation:

"Beware," she whispers and sighs. "Your sins will find you out."

There's righteous indignation in her voice. I smile, almost expecting her to shout "Halleluiah, Lord!"

I feel overbearing toward my parents, I feel protective of them, and I feel a need to mother them, something they will hear nothing of. When did I go from being their child, the one they cared for and worried about, to feeling responsible for them? Was there a period in between when we felt as equals? I don't remember. The period when I was the child segued seamlessly into the period when they need my help.

Later in the evening, I go back to my room. My parents go to bed early. I am ready to collapse. But sleep doesn't come: my diurnal clock is on U.S. time. I read long into the night and sleep almost until noon. After a frugal lunch, and while my parents nap, I go for a walk.

I didn't grow up in this well-to-do part of town, but I remember it from childhood. I walk on the beach where the houses are built close to the water. I look across Aarhus Bay, a wide shallow expanse that now, I am told, is quite polluted. On the other side are the green hills of the peninsula of Mols. I remember the folk stories of its people, the Molbos that I heard growing up:

The country was at war; the enemy was approaching. The Molbos wanted to hide their beautiful church bell.

"No problem," said Jeppe. "Let me take it out to sea and bury it at the bottom of Aarhus Bay."

" How will we ever find it again?" his fellow Molbos asked.

"Oh, that's easy," said Jeppe. "I will just carve a notch on the railing of the boat where I put it down.

I walk among the kelp so casually heaped onto the beach. The hedges of dog roses surrounding the houses on the beach are blooming: beautiful red and white blooms that in fall will carry the succulent hips. I remember times, when I was little, going to visit my father's friends who had a house here on the beach and canoeing on the Bay with their boys. Somewhat later, these same people moved to another house, an enormous estate it seemed, not far from my parents' present apartment. I remember visiting and being over-whelmed by the sheer number of rooms in the house, believing my father's friends to be enormously rich. As I think back, I realize they were ordinary middle class people running a manufacturing business out of an old patrician villa that was falling apart around them. How easily one is deceived in child-hood, I think. Then, things are magical and larger-than-life. As one grows older one seems to loose the capacity to be mystified.

I walk along the beach to the woods where the beech trees are budding. Wild leeks cover the forest floor and the smell of onions fills my nostrils. As children, we had walked through these woods to go swimming in summer or skating in winter.

As I walk here I happen to think of my mother's jealousy as I experi-enced it in Aden and as my parents have related it to us in their memoirs. I wonder what stoked the fires of my mother's pathological jealousy. Did she have reason to be jealous? I think not. My father was a loving and at-tentive husband whose only fault was his excruciating honesty. My parents had made a point of telling us about the missionary nurse who pursued our father, about his attraction to Mrs. Walker, and about the jealousy that had intruded upon the happiness of their early years together. It had been an ef-fort for them, I could tell from their writing, to admit to their children the presence of the dark shadow that had loomed over their early, married life. Jealousy had repeatedly besieged Eleanor, they said, she had fought it val-iantly, and together they had worked on maintaining a mutual trust.

I think of the time in Aden in 1951 when my mother—she was fifty-four years old then—had had a spat of jealousy in the car in front of her children. Why had this issue reappeared between my parents? Was menopause creating havoc with my mother's emotions? I sincerely doubt that any sense of inferior-ity lay at the root of her behavior. My mother cared little about her appear-ance, vanity was of the devil, and I also doubt she felt intellectually inferior. She was outspoken, and was unafraid to voice her opinion, sometimes paying little regard to the appropriateness of her comment or the propitiousness of the moment. Yet, why did she react the way she did? Was it because she had not been part of my father's life from 1937–'39 and from 1946–'48? Was she jealous of the past he shared with these women missionaries? I know little about my parents' sexual relationship, but my mother often enough—directly and indirectly—expressed her distaste for men's sexual appetites and I suspected that she felt that sexual relations was something to endure, not to enjoy.

I return to my parents' apartment for dinner. Mum and Dad help each other with the preparations, though Dad does most of the actual work. It is basic Danish cooking, meat and potatoes, gravy, and sometimes some over-cooked vegetables. They refuse my offer to cook, afraid that I will come up with something unusual, something too spicy.

That night before going to bed, I go to the lecture hall in the nursing home. All the lights are off and in the dark I fumble for the switches. The lecture hall is far away from the residents' rooms and I know I will disturb no one. I sit down at the piano and play and sing from the hymnbooks and the books of Danish national songs lying in the piano bench. I go from one to the other, savoring the words and the melodies. I love the patriotic songs, but wonder if I would feel as strongly about them had I not left Denmark. They evoke all that is good about my country. When I play them at home in America—as I often do—I feel a longing for Denmark and the Danish way of life, but somehow I have the feeling that the Denmark I am singing about has nothing to do with its present-day equivalent. I suspect the songs, even at their writing, were but expressions of longing for something that didn't exist anymore.

The days slip by. We talk, we reminisce. My parents tell me about their missionary friends, the ones I knew, many of them dead now. They talk about Aden. Of course, the work my parents and their co-workers did there has long since ceased. When Aden became independent in 1967 the colonists were ousted and with them the missionaries. The life they lived there is now in the distant past, but I treasure talking with my parents about my past, about my roots.

A Joyful Time

One day while I am visiting my parents I take the rental car and head north out of the city. The road follows the shoreline of the Bay of Aarhus; summerhouse colonies eventually give way to open fields. About thirty miles out I see the small town of Rønde up ahead; it has grown over the years and is now spilling down the southern slope of the long hill.

Once in town I stop across from a large red brick building, Rønde Gymnasium, the boarding school I attended from 1954 to 1956. Much has changed here; buildings have been added and it is no longer a private Christian Gymnasium, but a public school. So much happened while I was there; events that became riveted in my memory forever. I walk around town, past the cinema, the hotel, the Youth Hostel, and the bakery. Then I drive down to the ruins of the old Kalø Castle to which my schoolmates and I walked many an afternoon.

I have known this area since I was little; my family spent wartime summers at a nearby beach, Følle Strand, in a tiny summerhouse, a bunkhouse really, with no conveniences. We bathed in the waters of the bay where the shallow beach was filled with wading birds at low ebb. With no kitchen, Mum cooked outside and here she also washed our clothes. On hot summer days, we walked to the beach through narrow lanes where bees buzzed among the wild flowers and the tall bordering grass, and waded far out, slipping on rounded rocks and kelp to reach a sandy bottom. Horse flies flew a zigzag course around our wet bodies.

I had gone to school in Copenhagen the first year I was back in Denmark. We lived in the suburb of Valby and daily I biked to the school in the center of Copenhagen. It is hard to describe how excited I was during this period. I had not thought it possible there could be so much to learn; it was as if my schooling in Aden had taught me nothing. Only someone so deprived of learning can appreciate the hunger I felt about acquiring knowledge. Not only could I learn at school—it was an accelerated course designed to teach the entire middle school curriculum in one year—but the presence of libraries allowed me to immerse myself in world literature and a huge new world opened up to me. When after a year my parents prepared to return to Aden, they enrolled me at a boarding school for an accelerated two years of the Gymnasium. The Mathematical-Scientific Line—the most appropriate for my further studies—was not offered at Rønde Gymnasium. This pleased me no end since I was therefore forced to choose the Modern Languages Line where my inclination lay. Languages came easy to me, I enjoyed studying them, and I graduated in English, German, French, Latin, and Swedish.

Sending me to a boarding school was the best choice my parents could have made for me and I am eternally grateful to them for not placing me in a home with friends as they did with my sisterAnna.

As I walk around the ruins on the tiny island of Kalø I think of evenings in early spring spent here with my first love. We found our way across the causeway in the dark, on a tiny path on the dyke, and waited for the moon to rise before approaching the crumbling walls of the old castle.

The time I knew him had been a calm and joyful time. I had met him a few weeks into the school year. He was tall and slender, his hair dark and wiry; I remember how his eyes followed me everywhere. His intense scrutiny unsettled me. I wasn't used to such open, but silent interest from the other sex. What did he want? He was an upper-class man and I had not expected interest from that quarter.

1954. My parents bring me to the boarding school a week after I turn seventeen. I join a crowd of young people moving in with their parents' help. To my delight, I find that my roommate and I will share two rooms on the third floor, one of the rooms the size of a large closet. As I explore the rooms, in floats a petite girl. Moving with grace, head perched on an elongated neck, she curtsies as she gives hand to my parents. She is Kirsten, the one who will share my rooms with me.

Together we survey the room. Our stuff is piled on the floor and as I wonder where to begin, Kirsten says:

"I like the small room. It's perfect for me. I like to be cozy."

Quickly and gracefully—she is a ballet dancer I later learn—she glides in and out of the tiny cubicle managing to find space for all her things in the small cupboard, under her bed, and on her desk. I unpack my summer clothes and place them in the chest-of-drawers I have brought. My winter clothes are in the carved Chinese cedar chest my parents bought me in Egypt; that and a leather puff—also bought there—will be my constant companions during the following years, reminders of the world I left. Awkwardly my father helps me as my mother gives last minute advice.

I listen with half an ear; I am anxious for my parents to leave so I can get to know Kirsten.

Cheerfully I hug them, unmindful that I will not see them again for another two years.

One day he comes up to me. Cradling his pipe in his left hand, he introduces himself.

"Hi, I'm Bent."

I blush, revealing, I think, that I have asked around and know his name already.

"I'm Martha," I offer my hand. His is bony, his fingers long and slender.

"How is school?"

"I love it here." I want to tell him how much, but I hold back, feeling shy.

"Do you want to go for a walk with me tonight?" he asks. His smile is lopsided; maybe it is because of the pipe, but I find it attractive.

Surprising myself I say: "Oh, yes, I'd love to."

We meet outside the school. As we walk down the hill the setting autumn sun casts golden rays on the stubbly, already harvested grain fields, lending luminosity to the yellow leaves on trees along the road. I wonder what to say to him. I know his name, but nothing else, and I am a stranger to small talk.

He asks about my family.

He is trying to put me at ease and he doesn't realize it is the last thing I want to talk about, I think. My family is like no one else's. Nobody has missionary parents.

As I tell him my parents are in Arabia, I realize he knows already.

"Don't you miss them?" he asks, "I think I'd miss my parents if they were that far away."

I am quietly amazed. At seventeen, I have thought it unsophisticated to miss one's parents.

"Not really," I say, as yet unaware that school vacation with no home to go to will change that. Yet, does he understand, I wonder, how much I enjoy being on my own. I am happy my parents are far away. Family is not important right now.

"How was it living in Arabia?"

How can I begin to tell him what the desert was like, how funny Abdullah was, how I felt about my school mates marrying at age fourteen. He cannot possibly understand my life there, I think. Nor can he understand my passion about the place, a passion I think people will somehow find strange. I feel one has to see and experience the desert to understand its beauty. Searching for words, I try to tell him, all the while thinking to myself: Why did I agree to this walk? I must be boring him. What does he expect? That I am fascinating because I have lived in a foreign country? That will be too much to live up to. Yet how can I explain to someone who has grown up in this lush, tidy, pretty country how wondrous Aden is despite its poverty, aridness, and overwhelming heat? How captivating are the smells of its markets—the smells of frankincense, ginger, and coffee? How crowded and colorful are its streets with the many people, goats, donkeys, and camels? How beautiful its people?

I shiver and hug myself in the cool September night. Stars pierce the blue-black sky. The only artificial light comes from the school, on the hill far behind us. A half moon now peers through the leaves of the trees along the lane and cast wan shadows across the road.

"Maybe we should go back," I say.

"Hey, you're cold! Here. Take my jacket."

I feel awkward, but do not want to refuse his offer.

He helps me into the jacket and puts his arms around my shoulders. We walk on in silence. I feel the warmth of his body. Happiness bubbles up inside me, surging up from deep inside. Tentatively I put my arm around his slender muscular waist, looking up at him, smiling.

How wonderful to hold someone close, I think joyously. How wonderful that someone cares about me.

Before we turn back, he stops and kisses me.

We fell in love and spent all our free time together. In the evenings, Bent played the piano in the student lounge. I sat in a corner with my friends, quiet, and full of wonder. He loves me, I thought. The lounge was full, the students loud, but through it all I heard his music; he played by ear. Every recess we spent together; nothing existed for us but each other. Sneaking out at night, we roamed the country lanes or walked to the beach where at the bottom of the bay we watched the moon rise behind the ruins of the castle. On weekends, we went to dances at the youth hostel. I had never danced before, but how I loved Bent holding me as we danced to "How Much Is that Doggy in the Window?" and—I thought later—other equally inane songs. Bent was loving, sincere, and gentle with me. I felt secure and appreciated; I felt nothing could ever shatter the dreamy intensity of this my first love.

Then, that spring, I received the news that my sister Elin, a student nurse, had attempted suicide. I was devastated at the thought of the pain she must have suffered. I wanted to go to Copenhagen to visit her in the hospital, but could not afford to. What had happened to my cheerful, outgoing sister? I suffered through days of concern. As I was unable to call her, I wrote.

Some time after her discharge, Elin came to visit and treated me to coffee at the hotel. She appeared to be back to her normal self, her smile sunny as ever. As we ordered coffee and cake, Elin lit a cigarette.

"I feel good now," she said, eyes sparkling, blond hair framing her heart shaped face. I really loved Elin; she was so beautiful and sincere. Yet, I had many questions about what had happened. At twenty-two how could Elin not want to live? She had all her life before her.

She talked about how she often became despondent—seemingly with-out cause—yet at other times she would feel upbeat and feel she could tackle anything. She had taken pills. A roommate found her.

I hardly knew what to say and we sat in silence for a while, sipping our coffee. A May fly buzzed in the window, repeatedly throwing itself against the glass, looking for a way to escape out into the pale spring day.

"I am getting to accept that it's how I am," Elin finally said. "The psychi-atrist wanted me on lithium. I refused." She said this with a cocky smile.

"Why?" I asked.

"At times I feel so great. I am on top of the world and full of energy. I can accomplish anything I want," she drank the last of her coffee. "Medication would affect my mood, make it more stable, the psychiatrist says—make it more dull, I say."

Elin is often enigmatic, I thought, when she had left. She had been temperamental as a child, and opinionated and outspoken as she grew old-er. Nevertheless, she was a wonderfully caring person—a good nurse, I felt sure—yet those mood swings were disconcerting. Wouldn't balance, being on an even keel, be a better way to happiness? How could she stand the roller-coaster rides?

When summer vacation came, Kirsten and I found temp work in Copenha-gen. We shared the house of Kirsten's uncle while he was away. Frequent-ly alone there, as Kirsten worked the opposite shift, I often felt lonesome and isolated, not always sure what I was lonesome for. Sometimes I read for hours; sometimes I thought about Aden and, remembering the beauty of the sun setting behind Al-Bureiqa, I could almost smell the sand and the heat. When the birds woke me in the morning, I remembered how the muezzins' call to prayer had woken me in Aden. Yet, though I longed for the sounds, the smells, and the warmth of the climate, I knew I did not want to be there with my parents. Aden was not for me now.

At the end of summer, Bent came to Copenhagen to start the bike trip we had planned together. I had looked forward to seeing him, but there was something strange about meeting him again in this environment. I had been very lonesome in the city, yet I had hardly missed him. Despite my initial misgivings the two of us set off on the bike trip. We biked from Copenhagen back to Jutland, staying at Youth Hostels along the way. It was late in the season; many of the hostels were empty except for us.

At one hostel, the solitude of the empty women's dormitory was oppressive; like a heavy weight, it settled on my chest. I was sleepless and continued to be lonesome, not for my family, not for anyone, not for Bent. What do I want, I thought as I struggled to sleep. What do I want with my life? What do I want with Bent? Do I even want a future with him? I wasn't sure I wanted to be with him. Yet, when we reached his parents' home I had almost convinced myself I was still in love with him.

As I sit here in 1981, I look across the shallow bay of Kalø Vig. The tide is out now. The gray sandy bottom on which are staked rows of old fishing nets, stretches far into the bay. I think of how ambivalent I felt about many things then—in 1954—and how I always felt a need to move on. I think of how everything here at Kalø Vig is so minute in scale—across the small bay are Mols Bakker, the hills we had biked to and hiked in as students—and so immutable; the castle at Kalø has been left in ruins since 1672. Such permanency, I think; a permanency we neither understand nor appreciate in youth. Only when older, do we feel a need for permanency, only then do we appreciate being connected to not only our past but our country's past.

The Gymnasium had been good for me. Here I had gained independence and confidence, and here I had experienced the happiness of a first love. But the idyll was not to last. Within weeks of my returning to school in 1955 something happened that changed our family's world into before and after.

Fall from Grace

When I arrive back at my parents' apartment for dinner I find my brother there. Johs lives alone in a small apartment a block away. He is a daily visitor at our parents' home, frequently taking in a meal with them, and when I am home, I visit him in his flat.

Johs greets me with a smile.

He is now fifty and I think about how much he looks like the older Johannes Brahms, stocky, bald, with a large graying beard. Johs is mostly sedentary now and his increasing paunch bears witness to that. He is always quiet and pleasant, yet invariably I become sad when I see him. He is but a shadow of his former self now and I always grieve for the person he never became.

"How are you, Johs?" I ask.

"Hungry," he mumbles without meeting my gaze.

As I set the table for dinner, I think of how little I knew Johs when we were growing up. My memories of him from then are hazy; he is older than I am and he had been away at boarding school for two years. I remember him best from after our return from Aden. By then he had dropped out of college and was serving his military duty near Copenhagen. I remember how tall, at six feet he is the tallest in our family, handsome, and slim he was in his uniform. He came home on weekends, where he went about saying little, and sleeping much.

I think of a ride Johs and I took together in 1954. If Johs wasn't so pre-occupied now, I would remind him of that trip many years ago. It is so vivid in my mind. I want to ask him. Do you remember this the way I remember it?

Do you remember the wind in our hair as we traveled north on your motor-cycle? I had my arms around you. Though you had just bought this bike, I trusted you. It was October. You were twenty-three, I was seventeen. We were going north, I to see my boyfriend and his family, you to see Anna. You had picked me up at the boarding school. You knew about boarding schools, you said, you had liked yours. As you said it I thought, maybe it had been good for you to get away from four sisters, from our family's crowded house; it had allowed you independence, and allowed you to do boy things. You had been a grown boy of fifteen, ready to face the world.

Do you remember how we traveled along a country road? The day was cool, the leaves turning. I was warmly dressed, but I hid behind your strong back to keep out of the wind. We stopped at the bottom of a large hill and drank hot tea from thermoses. You had just finished your military duty and now you were teaching at a country school on a small island. You told me about the island. One could walk around it in an hour. There were only about twenty families there. You lived in an apartment above the one-room school. It was lonely; sometimes you went stir crazy, you said. If it hadn't been for the people who invited you to their homes now and then, you didn't think you could stand it. But you were happy now it was *kartoffelferie*—po-tato vacation—and you could get away.

I remember your smile as we sat in the ditch sharing some *wienerbrød*. I told you about my new love. You were envious. You talked about your broken engagement. You didn't understand what happened. You pulled at the grass straws that were still green; you stared at the ground. Around us the fields were plowed and dark, except the potato fields, whose wizened plants awaited the forks. One day I was in love with a young woman who wanted to marry me, you said; the next day she was gone. This was two years before, but you couldn't forget. I smiled. I didn't understand your pain. A young man loved me and I was deliriously happy. You will find someone else, Johs, I said. You looked at me, doubtful, yet wanting to believe me.

Johs has turned on the radio, ostensibly to listen to the news. Whether he listens or not is open to question. How bittersweet that memory is, I think as I finish setting the table. That trip was the last time we were together with hope uniting us; a year later things had changed.

1955. It is late August, just two weeks after my return to Rønde Gymnasium. I now occupy a single room across the hall from the rooms I shared with Kirsten. A smell of burnt Bakelite emanates from my recently turned off radio. Forever after I will associate this smell with what happened that year.

Johs had been staying alone at a friend's farm on the isolated North Sea coast during the last weeks of summer. Having decided to go back to school, he was now on his way to the teacher's college he had enrolled at—or so at least I surmised—when he again stopped to see me at the boarding school.

"They want to shoot me…," he says.

"Shoot you?"

"Yes, some neighbors…at the farm…want to shoot me."

As he speaks, he paces, his steps mechanical and measured, his voice without inflection.

"Nobody has guns in Denmark anymore, it's peacetime now, Johs," I say. His comments are ludicrous and his demeanor frightening.

Fresh air and wind has browned his face. Disheveled sun-streaked tangles of hair fall over his already receding hairline; he combs them back with his fingers, silent. Cradling his pipe and continuing his pacing he takes out his tobacco pouch, refills his pipe, and lights it. His eyes are dull and unfocused. He mumbles to himself.

"Johs, please sit down and talk to me. This is nonsense. Of course no one wants to shoot you."

"Oh, yes…," he says," it's true."

I stare at him in disbelief. He really means this? Yet, it doesn't make sense. Denmark is a peaceful nation. People don't just shoot one another.

"No, really…," he continues in a monotone, "they are talking to me… right now…telling me they will kill me…."

I feel my chest tighten.

"What do you mean 'talking to you'? Who are they?"

"One is a doctor…he lives next to the farm. These past two weeks he has been threatening me…constantly…"

Students run down the hall to their classes, but it barely registers with me.

"What do you mean…? I guess I don't understand, Johs."

"Right now…he and the other man are talking to me…telling me they want to kill me…."

"But how can they be talking to you now? They are on the North Sea."

"I hear their voices...I don't see them. I just hear their voices...their voices are inside my head...," he stops, bewildered. "They scare me...."

"Johs, how can you hear their voices in your head?"

"I don't know...but I do."

He really believes this, I think. How can he? Somehow, I sense that something is terrifyingly wrong. His reality has changed dramatically and somehow I know, deep within me, that this is something momentous, some huge dark shadow that will never go away. I try to listen to him. I don't know what to say or do.

In the stillness that follows, I feel dislocated. Sunshine filters through the green leaves outside my window framing him with speckled light as he paces. The muted sounds of children playing in the street reach me...happy and joyful sounds while within my room a world is crumbling.

When dinner is over, I sit down with my needlework. My parents will not let me do the dishes; they hardly let me into the kitchen now that they know I scrutinize everything. Johs goes back to his apartment; he is more distant than usual and prefers being alone.

I take him to our family doctor, Dr. Aggebo, in Aarhus. We sit in his office, Johs agitated and anxious. As he tells Dr. Aggebo about the men who want to kill him I feel paralyzed. All I register is the tapping of his feet on the floor, the up-and-down movements of his knees, and the batting of his eyelids. Dr. Aggebo's large jowls and red cheeks jiggle as his sonorous voice fills the room.

"...admission...State Hospital..." is all I hear. In my mind—as if in a daze— I visualize this place I remember from childhood: beautiful grounds, lawns and trees, orchards, vegetable gardens, and...strange, broken people...raking the grass...hoeing the potatoes...pulling the weeds...standing with their hands on garden tools, staring into space, mumbling to themselves; old, dark buildings...nurses in blue and white uniforms...doctors in lab coats.

We left Dr. Aggebo's office, took the bus to the State Hospital where we, two forlorn figures, Johs twenty-four and I eighteen, walked through its gates, a prison it seemed, with fences all around. I felt empty. Unable to think, I responded mechanically to questions as the staff checked Johs in. Everyone was kind, I am sure, but I do not remember what happened next, or how I got back to school. Dr. Aggebo said he would write our parents once there was a diagnosis; until then, he insisted, I must keep everything to myself. I had not questioned Dr. Aggebo's authority and I spoke to no one about Johs's illness, nor did I confide in my diary.

As I think of all this, I wonder how the physician could possibly have asked that of me. What a burden to put on a young woman's shoulders. How had I even made it through that time. I remember so little of those first days, I must have banished them from memory. Weeks later I learned that Johs had paranoid schizophrenia. I had a dream then:

Schizophrenia...I taste the word...paranoid schizophrenia...I want to spit it out; it twists around my tongue. I try to rid myself of it, I tear it out of my mouth, throw it out the window, into the garbage, hide it in a cupboard, but always it reappears, pursues me, like a train bearing down on me, schizophrenia...schizophrenia...schizophrenia...

After that, everything changed for me. My relationship with Bent was an indulgence, I decided, almost a frivolity, and I wrote him saying I could no longer see him, giving no explanation; it was as if I needed to rid myself of all selfish emotional ties. Instead, I became focused and disciplined, yet reckless, as I threw myself into an affair with an older student, an intellectual, I thought, but soon lost heart, broke it off and let schoolwork consume me. Ambitiously I strove for the highest grades.

I felt aloof, callous, and seemingly without feelings. Elin, still a student nurse in Copenhagen, came to my rescue after the first week. She and I were very intellectual about it all, very adult. We wrote reassuring letters to our parents in Aden encouraging them to finish their term and not leave precipitously: "the doctors are doing all they can." Such trust we had in the doctors who had so little to offer. Elin and I wanted to shield our parents.

And every Wednesday I visited Johs. I still remember the strident November rain that year, how it lashed at me as I walked to the State Hospital from the bus. Persistent westerly winds whipped across the country and stripped the trees of leaves. My hair was tousled and wet, my cheeks red as I sat talking to him.

"They put a radio in my teeth…," he tells me.

"Who?"

"The people who talk to me…inside my head."

"That's not possible, Johs."

"Oh, yes it is…it's a tiny radio."

I try not to argue with him, and usually I don't ask who "they" are. "They" have now become a familiar concept between us, almost like family. Mumbling, or talking aloud, Johs has ongoing conversations with "them," the voices.

We are sitting in a high-ceilinged room with tall windows and mustard colored curtains. In the background, patients sit around tables or in lounge chairs, in an eerie quiet, interrupted only by occasional outbursts. Seated in a brown, worn chair Johs stares straight ahead, unlit pipe in mouth, his face immobile, disturbed only by occasional rapid batting of his droopy lids. He is like a zombie.

"I hate the electro-shock therapy," he says. "They strap me to a table, put electrodes to my head, a rubber thing in my mouth, I can't stand it…and afterwards I remember nothing…I don't want to go through another one…."

"Things will get better, Johs," I say.

Yet things did not get better.

Year after year, he took the pills. Ten, fifteen, twenty-five a day; carefully meted out by the Public Health Nurse in Monday's slot in his medicine box…Tuesday's…Wednesday's…and so on. The drugs calmed his anxiety, but left him sedated.

After our parents returned from Aden in 1956 he lived with them for a decade, first at the country school where our father taught, then in their house in Aarhus. When they moved to the apartment, he moved into rented rooms, but for some years now he has been in his present apartment, not far from our parents; I often visit him there.

His life is a life of monotony. Day after day he sits there. Outside the apartment, on a small balcony with flower boxes, are a chair, a table, and an umbrella, inviting him outside; but he prefers the inside. He sits behind the blinds and the red curtains, in an old chair, the arms worn through by the constant rotating motion of his hands, pipe in mouth. Old worn furniture crowds the room; a beech-wood desk—a relic from his childhood, marred by ink spills and burn holes—stands by the window, the bed is in a back corner. Smoke has stained the ceiling and walls dark. Photographs and pictures are tacked to the wall between framed pictures of "The Great White Host" and "The Suffering Christ." Along one wall are two bookcases, one stacked on top of the other, overflowing with books, tapes, a boom box, and newspapers. In the small kitchen, the coffee pot gives off the smell of constantly brewing, constantly concentrating coffee, coffee that by the end of the day is like syrup. When I visit in the morning, Johs is often in bed after a sleepless night. The television is blaring to drown out the voices.

Once he tells me about his friend, the young pastor. Depression cost him his job, and his family. He was alone. The two of them talked about Kierkegaard. The young pastor eventually committed suicide. Johs, almost envious of him, did not question why.

As my thoughts return to 1955, I think of the person I then became. My brother's illness shattered my faith in God. How could God have let this happen? Johs was so amiable and kind. He would have made a good teacher, but he was never able to finish his degree, he never regained the presence of mind required to teach, and never married. He took no interest in anything and all his energies were centered on keeping those voices at bay, constantly trying to placate them, being unable to, and invariably falling prey to their threats. I often despaired at the emptiness of his gaze. The outer world did not concern him, he looked within himself, not with discernment, but in confusion, having no control over his inner world. During those first years I prayed repeatedly: "God please make Johs well, please make Johs well," but it was an empty mantra without meaning to me, because I no longer believed that God could or would grant me what I wanted for my brother.

To take my mind off Johs's illness, I immersed myself in my studies. In a strange way I felt focused and strong, energized almost, propelled forward. For better or for worse I became an adult. I felt I stood alone and only my own strength and not a supernatural force would sustain me. In some way my brother's illness steeled me, made me stronger.

Purpose filled me then, while I paid little attention to my feelings. That was dangerous territory, filled with despair and anger.

My parents have now finished the dishes and return to the living room with coffee and cookies. How much more at peace they are now with Johs's illness, I think.

After returning from Aden in 1956 they had, much to my relief, taken on the full burden of Johs's illness and the State Hospital had discharged him to their care. During the first years, they blamed themselves for not having been enough of a presence in Johs's life, for having sent him to boarding school, and for all they had not done. I remember many times when Johs could not sleep, when he panicked and sobbed that the voices, now emanating from the Royal Danish Court, threatened to burn him, that my parents held him in their arms, praying with him and for him until he slept. They bore their plight with stoicism. Eventually, however, they realized that nothing they had done or had not done would likely have changed Johs's fate.

Now in 1981, their worry is: "Who will watch over him when we die?" I, as so often, feel guilt that I am so far away, but I know my sisters, Frida and Elin, will care for him.

"Let us hear another chapter of the book," Mum says.

There are so many chapters in the book of my life, I muse, chapters that never finish, but continue without resolution. For now, however, I leave off at a paragraph in the chapter about my brother.

Life and Death

My days with my parents pass quietly, and all too soon, it is time to go home. This is always the hard part. An ocean separates us and I cannot easily return should they suddenly be taken ill. We tell each other that we fear we may never see each other again. It is good to be able to express this reality. Dad as always adds: "We may not see each other again here on earth, but we shall be united in Heaven." Do I believe that? When I think of my own death I imagine my body dissolving into molecules and atoms and returning to earth. I have difficulty imagining that I should shed my earthly remains while my spirit joins God. To me, mind and spirit are products of the body, products of brain activity, nerve cells, nerve endings, and synapses. How can my spirit continue to exist if my body has dissolved? The only continued existence of my spirit I can imagine is in the memory of the people who have known me, and that existence is not eternal. But I nod my assent. Little do I realize how much death is part of life and that soon thoughts about death will preoccupy me. Now, however, is not the time to have a discussion with my parents about life and death. In fact, I know I will never have that discussion. My views might devastate them.

Again Dad's voice shakes, his eyes fill with tears as he says good-bye. Mum, quiet, smiles.

I had gone to see the dermatologist, a colleague two months before because of the small black lesion I had noticed in the midline of my chest. I had watched it grow minimally over a period of months and had not thought much of it. The dermatologist took a biopsy.

"It's a malignant melanoma," he told me a week later and without mulling over the implications of this piece of bad news I had merely asked: "So what's the next step?"

Afterwards I wondered why I had accepted the diagnosis so easily. Though I knew melanomas were viciously malignant skin cancers, I just wanted the lesion dealt with. I felt sure it could not be very serious; the lesion was tiny, no more than a few millimeters; I was so healthy. How could something that tiny possibly threaten my life?

I had a wider excision and went to the Mayo Clinic for a second opinion. The Mayo physician initially thought nothing further needed to be done and I went off to Denmark to see my parents, convinced this little episode was behind me.

When I returned from Denmark the news awaited me that the melanoma was more serious than anticipated. I needed yet a wider excision. A pre-operative chest-x-ray at the Mayo Clinic showed a tumor in my chest. Probably a metastasis, we were told, but it could be something else. The only way to know was to take the tumor out. I latched on to the "something else" and felt calm and strangely removed from my situation.

When I woke up after the thoracotomy I found my husband sitting beside me. I noticed that his voice contained little of the worry of the last few days. He told me the tumor was benign (sarcoid). I was surprised. Did this mean that I mentally, though not emotionally, had accepted the diagnosis of metastasis? Not that it mattered; all that mattered was that things were much better than expected.

There were many telephone calls across the Atlantic during this time, from and to my sister Elin, from and to my parents. I became aware that Elin must have expressed something to the effect that the melanoma was a death sentence; my parents had therefore thought I was visiting them one last time before the cancer claimed me. This explained their solicitousness toward me during my visit, and my surgery confirmed for them the seriousness of my illness and they were convinced the surgeries were not the end of it. Anxiously they listened to my voice on the phone, trying to detect what I might not tell them.

At the time of my illness, I faced the possibility of dying with equanimity. During recovery I felt so tired that life had little interest for me. Had it not been for Hans and the children I would gladly have given myself up to death; the possibility of lapsing into nothingness was attractive. Yet, though I had doubts about the Hereafter, I was comforted by my father's letters and by the knowledge that Johs, my parents, and my parents' friends—though far away—prayed daily for my recovery.

Sometimes I wondered if my parents thought God had struck me with cancer for a reason. I balked at this. To me illness and death were random events. I did not believe that a loving God visited these scourges on people to teach them a lesson. I thought of all the babies I cared for as a neonatologist, and reflected on the ones who had died. How could one say that God willed his or her death. However, if parents found comfort in thinking that God had taken their children to Him because He had wanted them with Him in heaven, I did not see it as my mission to dissuade them, but I believed that such things happened because of accidents of nature.

Nonetheless, my parents' prayers comforted me. This was the comfort of unconditional love, I realized, the meaning of family. A parent's love sustains you in good times and buoys you through bad times, though I in my everyday life, thousands of miles away from my parents, had paid little attention to it.

The author's brother Johs, her father, Elin, Mummy, Anna, the author, and Frida at Følle Strand 1960.

Roots

(2002)

A Civilized Way

My husband and I are about to land in Copenhagen. It is June 2002. As we come in over Denmark from the northwest, I recognize Limfjorden, the fjord that cuts the "hat" off the peninsula of Jutland, and I almost imagine I can see our Danish home below. In a big swoop, we approach Copenhagen from the east, flying in over Øresund; an entire windmill park rises from its waters and towards the immediate south is the new bridge that connects Sweden to the rest of Europe. The red roofs of the city make me feel nostalgic and patriotic, a "pull" I always feel when I land here. This is my country—this Lilliputland.

By car, we backtrack to our farmhouse on a hill overlooking Limfjorden. We stop for food in the village; the grocer and his wife—both attractive, grey-haired, and in their early fifties—welcome us back. Some beer, snaps, rye bread, butter, and deli meat and we are set until the next morning. Then we drive down the gravel road where in front of us the fjord shimmers silvery-blue and there—on the hill—is the thatched whitewashed small farm, our Danish home.

As we drive up the sunken dirt road, the house beckons with red-and-white-gingham curtains. Through the green-painted door, we enter the low-beamed front room. We are home!

I sleep late the next morning and wake to the smell of coffee. Hans has been to the baker for fresh rolls and a Danish newspaper, and has already set the table. We savor the *rundstykker* (rolls), the lightly salted, yellow Danish butter, and the coffee and immerse ourselves in Danish news.

Together with Hans's parents, we had bought this farm in 1966 when we graduated from medical school. We had no money then, the farm was in a terrible state, and it had seemed an audacious undertaking, but over the years, the farm had been lovingly restored by my father-in-law, an architect. My husband's parents are now dead and Hans and I are sole owners of this small paradise.

We spend our days exploring the countryside. After thirty-five years here there are still new things to see: a new archeological dig from the Viking era, a reclusive artist's museum, the second-world-war German bunkers and museum on the North Sea coast, and new bike routes.

We drive to east Jutland and bike in the area where my father was born and raised. From his memoir, I know the name of the village of his birth. There I find a 300-year-old tiny yellow half-timbered house with a thatched roof overlooking the river. I am convinced this house is his birthplace, a fact later confirmed by a cousin.

"I was born on the longest day of the year, June 22 1897 [my father writes in his memoir]. My mother told me that she was outside sweeping at sundown when she went into labor. My father was not home; he had gone across the river to visit relatives in Terp. She therefore sent word to a farmer to drive to Tånum for the "madam" (the midwife)."

Supporting my bike, I stand next to the little yellow house and stare across the river where my grandfather had gone on the day of my father's birth more than a hundred years ago. This year at my cousin's I see for the first time a picture of this grandfather, a strikingly handsome young man with long blond hair combed back from his forehead. The picture is taken in profile. He looks upward and into the left of the picture; I am struck by the yearning in his face.

The green fields stretch down toward the small river that meanders through the meadows. The yellow house is tastefully restored; the half-timber a lustrous black; the new windows have tiny square double panes; no doubt the house has all modern amenities. I try to imagine what it would have been like for Dine, my grandmother, to live here so long ago, with five children. The house was likely in poor repair with drafty windows and doors, and no running water. She must have sent the children to fetch water from the well and to scoop up coal in the shed so she could heat the water and start up a fire to keep the house warm. Dine was an avid gardener later in life, but early on when she was alone with five children—her handsome husband had died four years after my father's birth—would her garden have been as neat as the one that surrounds the house presently?

I am amazed at the beauty of the landscape: the rolling hills and to the north the large lake, Fussingsø, where my namesake Andreas, my father's brother, went through the ice and drowned almost a century ago. At the end of it, a red-bricked castle peers through the tall beeches. About fifteen kilometers further west, south of the river, we ride past Skjern Manor House that with seven hundred acres on either side of the river had been my paternal great-great-grandparents. We stop at the tiny church that once belonged to the Manor. It was built in the twelfth century of granite ashlars and has no belfry. In its graveyard, I find tombstones engraved with my family name. Later, with the help of my genealogist cousin, I identify them all. I feel strangely connected to this landscape known to me from my father's description in a memoir of his grandparents, to the tiny church, and to the picturesque Manor House; these are my roots.

After a month of relaxation and visits with friends and family, Hans and I head back to Copenhagen stopping on the way in the small town of Sorø for the night. We dine in style at the Hotel Postgaarden and after dinner, we walk to the renowned Academy where my godparents' five rambunctious boys were students so many years ago. We walk through the Abbey portal, built in the twelfth century with Monk stone—a particularly large red brick—and onto the grounds of the Academy; the Chapel, the dormitories, and the classroom buildings are all three to four hundred years old. Sorø Lake is wind-tossed this evening, a fine mist obscures the opposite side, and on the near shore, weeping willows bend their branches to the water, submerging them. The town of Sorø has changed little and I recognize the square where the gig and horse were parked when we went on shopping expeditions with Aunt Lisbeth.

The next morning we drive north to the small town of Dianalund, another venture into our past. I had spent many a summer here, working at the large private mental and epileptic hospital, Kolonien Filadelfia, whose facilities are spread over about a hundred acres in a truly beautiful setting. Started in 1897 as an Epileptic Hospital, it later cared for epileptics as well as for patients with severe mental disorders. My father trained here as a deacon—a combination of nurse, social and pastoral worker—from 1918 to 1924 and for half a century my family had strong ties to the institution.

When I had first returned from Aden, I had worked here in housekeeping, dusting and cleaning floors in the nurses' and student nurses' rooms. My sister Elin was a student nurse here at the time, but often she worked nights and I saw little of her. I remember how lonely I had been and how much I had longed for Aden. Insomnia plagued me and I had been so depressed that I had sincerely doubted I would ever adjust to living in Denmark.

Hans and I drive through the grounds. So little has changed. Everything is tidy and well kept. With surprise we recognize the building where Hans, our son Michael, and I lived in 1963 when we were here on our first stint as substitute physicians; the building remains unchanged on the outside. In Denmark, people venerate buildings and do not tear them down when they no longer serve their original purpose. Later we come by the house we—or rather Michael, Peter, and I—lived in for six months. I worked here as a physician while Hans did his military obligations.

I recognize wards where I know my father worked during his training. They look the same as they did a hundred years ago, only the color is different. Of his first days here, my father, then twenty-one years old, wrote in his diary:

"I started my work at Filadelfia on November 15, 1918. I have my own room where on my weekly afternoon off and my every third Sunday off I can fire up the stove so the room is nice and cozy; I have never known such luxury.

Yet, there is no luxury in being a deacon-in-training. The salary is $2/month. The founder of the institution, Dr. Sell, preaches by example: his salary does not exceed $500/year.

I have been assigned to the floor with the least afflicted patients, Korshuset. I have quickly become accustomed to seeing epileptic fits that are at times truly frightening. We are only three deacons on this floor, responsible for about 40 patients."

December 13: "How wonderful it is to work here if only one can attain sufficient grace to give of oneself wholeheartedly. Just to get a smile out of others. It is indeed blessed to give....The Spanish Flue has announced its arrival among the female patients; many have become sick and some have died."

Sunday December 15: "This is 'trial by fire.' Yesterday afternoon three of our patients went to bed with a fever of 104°F, as did one of my colleagues. Now we are only two. By evening, two more patients were sick."

Monday evening, 10:30 p.m.: "We have 13 patients with the Spanish Flue. One patient has a temperature of 105°. The first patients to be taken ill [on the other wards] now seem on the mend. There were few quiet moments today. The Spanish cases get 15-25 camphor drops every 3 hours and a powder three times a day. My only remaining colleague, H.P., wants to take the call alone tonight. I hope he doesn't get ill, he has not been feeling well today."

Tuesday evening, 11:00 p.m.: "At 3 p.m. H.P. went home. His temperature this morning was 105° I had to manage alone except during mealtimes when Sørensen helped me. I had enough to do until 10 p.m. My legs are tired; otherwise I am well. I am glad Sørensen takes the call tonight. We now have 15 sick."

Later: "Wednesday and the following days Kristensen helped me. Friday night I hardly slept. Brøndum is very sick, he needs camphor injections [sic] every third hour. Saturday another deacon took over for me and I slept Saturday afternoon and night."

Sunday December 22: "Brøndum died last night. H.P. is worse—concern about pneumonia. Three other trainees and deacons are sick, Bach very bad."

What a different time then, I think. My father had just started his training, had no medical knowledge, yet he had to care for these very sick people. Of course, there was little one could have done for the Spanish Flue then. On the other hand, I think, the Spanish Flue might pose an even greater threat today as extensive global travel would spread it more rapidly than one could have imagined in 1918.

I am curious about how Kolonien Filadelfia functions today, and what type of patients are housed in these buildings. Most epileptics are now treatable and can live normal lives. I wish I had the time to immerse myself here again. Sometimes at home in the U.S. when I lose myself in a book about this place and in the pictures in it from the 1920's, I imagine my father in 1918 getting up in early morning, first shivering in the cold room then warming as he does his morning exercises, hastily making his way on a muddy gravel road to the ward where patient upon patient with the Spanish Flue awaits him. I see him here, in his white uniform, going from person to person in the large wards where wide pillars separate contiguous areas, each of which contains eight to ten white metal framed beds.

My father's training prepared him for what was to become his mission in life: preaching the gospel and taking care of people. Caring for others was one of the many values he instilled in his children; no wonder then that two of them became nurses, and one a doctor.

Hans and I now make our way past the Dianalund Nerveanatorium, an adjoining though separate facility where I had been a patient in 1957, the spring I had my first major depression. It was then a hospital for patients with "nervous" disorders, but it is not evident what it now is used for. Memories flood through me. Though it had been a distressing time in my life I think of my stay here with a certain fondness. I was bruised and hurt, and what good fortune it was for me to be nursed back to health in this beautiful environment. I remember so clearly my feelings during that spring of my twentieth year.

1957. I enroll at the medical faculty at Aarhus University in September of '56 after graduating from the Gymnasium.

Fall semester passes smoothly. I settle into university life. Some of my classmates from the Gymnasium study at the university, and others have enrolled at Teachers' Colleges in Aarhus. We meet in the evenings in our rooms over tea, coffee, and a biscuit—none of us have any money—and have long serious discussions or share unimportant anecdotes about our days, talking long into the night. We commiserate as we adjust to new and greater demands.

Then shortly after winter vacation, I become ill. Dr. Aggebo comes to see me. I have a fever and a sore throat. Mononucleosis, he tells me; it will take me a while to recover.

Yet, the days turn to weeks, winter slips into spring, and I sense no improvement. A deep fatigue settles in my body. Insidiously and imperceptibly, things begin falling apart. I drag myself to lectures, but am unable to concentrate and am too tired to stay at my studies for long. I become convinced I cannot catch up, I sink into deep hopelessness and sleep for hours on end. My enthusiasm, motivation, goals, and drive seem to have evaporated. A mocking voice within me says: so you thought you could do this? Where is the stamina in which you pride yourself? You don't have what it takes.

Nonetheless, I remain in school for another two months, daily hoping for improvement.

Finally, I give up and move home, but nothing changes. My parents, already coping with one child's mental illness, are at a loss, and how can they possibly help me, I think. They pray for me, but I myself have lost my faith in God. Since Johs's illness, I have withdrawn from any communion with Him. Not that I blame God, Johs was predisposed for his illness, and besides, I think it vainglorious of humans to believe that God, if he exists, is concerned with the individual. In desperation, I think: just stop all the praying and help me instead.

One day I find myself in the center of Copenhagen. I want to visit a bookstore, though I can hardly concentrate enough to read. Returning on a packed tram, standing on the back platform, I am crushed into a corner. I can't breathe, I think, heart pounding in my chest; if I don't get out now, I'll lose my mind. My mind plays tricks on me, tells me the situation calls for panic, and though I know that nothing will happen, I cannot convince my brain or my body. I claw my way through the mass of people, and finally I am on the sidewalk, breathless, pulse hammering. Safe? Maybe.

Sometimes I feel suffocated like this by the pressure I feel from my parents to be what they want me to be. I feel they don't accept me as I am. To me, at this stage of my life, their love seems so filled with conditions. If you love me, you will also love God; if you love me, you will go to church; if you love me, you will do what God wants you to do. All these tangles crowd me. I want to follow my own path, want to experience life on my own terms, and I do not want to be caught up in the web of my parents' conditions. Yet I do not want to tell them this. If I do, I will certainly lose their love. Maybe my parents will only love me as a child of God!

I, however, know nothing of parenthood yet, and not until I have children of my own, do I realize that parents love their children unconditionally. My parents would never have placed conditions on their love for me. Yet at this time I feel sure that they can never again be the comfort to me they were when I was young.

I walk the sidewalks of the posh Copenhagen suburb where missionaries on home-leave live in old patrician villas. My eyes blank, I scarcely register that spring is on its way, that snowdrops and crocuses are emerging from the ground, while buds burst large and plump from the surrounding bushes.

Finally, a doctor recommends hospitalization, and my father takes me to the place he knows best.

We arrive at the Sanatorium, a pleasant three story red brick building at the edge of a forest, surrounded on three sides by well-tended lawns.

A nurse shows me to a room with two beds. Romance novels, lipstick, toothpaste, brush, and comb on the night table reveal that someone occupies the second bed. I hang my clothes in the cupboard behind the door, undress, and sink into bed pulling the covers over my head. The room is quiet; a window is ajar. Outside the sun shines brilliantly, birds flutter and twitter in the tall beeches, but my world is muted and veiled in shades of gray.

At lunchtime, a nurse comes to my bedside.

"Would you want to come to the dining room to eat?"

"No, thank you," I say, sure I cannot. I want to stay where I am. How can I face all those strangers who may all be crazy?

Walking slowly, her shoulders drooping, the woman in the other bed returns to the room. Her face is broad, thick straight bangs cover her forehead; one thick long braid snakes down her back. Though young, her body seems strangely inert and tired. She glances at my bed, saying nothing. Disrobing she gets into bed.

A while later she asks:

"What's your name?" Her speech is slow and carries the intonation of the local dialect. I tell her.

"You'll like it here," she says.

Maybe, I think. But it doesn't matter. Sadness weighs so heavily on me, like a vise it grips my chest, so tight it hurts, and I don't care where I am. I just want to sleep in order to escape the pain.

When nighttime comes, however, I am still wide-awake in the darkness of the unfamiliar place. Light peeks under the door from the dimly lit hallway. I find my way to the toilets that smell oppressively of brown soap. The bathroom and the water closet with its overhead cistern are scrupulously clean, the toilet paper coarse and brown. The clanging of the chain as I flush resonates in the quiet, high-ceilinged room. Back in the hall, I see a nurse at a desk, a shaded lamp bathes her white figure in light.

"Everything OK?" she whispers.

"I can't sleep."

"I'll bring you a sleeping pill."

This buys me oblivion for a few hours.

The doctor's room at the Sanatorium is clean and uncluttered, the walls white with bright prints. Light streams through the large south facing windows. Outside on the lawn patients huddle on benches, smoking. I close my eyes to the brightness. I want to go back to the darkness of my north facing room. I have come to the appointment with the psychiatrist in my robe, and now I sit gingerly at the edge of a chair. The doctor has glasses and blond hair on a balding head. Impassively he sits behind a white table, not smiling, but looking kind.

"What has been going on with you?"

I raise my shoulders in uncertainty. What can I tell him? I don't know how to give an account in a cohesive way; how can I explain the total confusion I feel? How can I explain my lack of connection with reality, my inability to concentrate, to remember what happened yesterday, a week ago, a month ago. He scribbles in the shorthand notebook in front of him and when done he settles back in his chair expectantly. He is waiting for me to tell him more, I think, but I have no more to say. He then questions me about my parents, my siblings. I answer in monosyllables. I don't want to tell him about Johs. I feel branded by Johs's illness and worry that I myself may be next in line; in fact, I am petrified that I may be developing schizophrenia, and don't want the doctor to confirm my suspicions. All I tell him is that my brother is schizophrenic, diagnosed a year ago. The doctor notes this with nonchalance. I often try not to think about Johs; I cannot bear to contemplate him or his illness. I am unable to feel anything about it, except this one thing: a debilitating fear, that schizophrenia may affect me too.

The silence in the consultation room chokes me. Every minute is like an eternity. When is he done? I clutch my soaked handkerchief as tears trickle down my cheeks.

He prescribes an anti-depressant, which sedates me and relieves some of my anxiety, but does nothing for my feelings of despair, and the fatigue is excruciating. I feel life has nothing in store for me; I am now sure I will never become a doctor. I cry often.

The days are mild now. I lie staring at wispy clouds high in the sky. The doctor has prescribed that I rest outside every afternoon, whatever the weather. An attendant tucks me to the chin in warm blankets, so tight I can barely move. Smothered and pacified, I think ruefully, like my parents' smothering. They want to keep me safe, on the straight and narrow, close to God, afraid, as they are, that the world may contaminate me. Is their need to smother us children the result of their limited horizon and their, in particular my mother's, intense fear of the secular world? I have often sensed that my mother is fearful she herself may succumb to the temptations of the world. Proudly she declares that she is not vain lest she become conceited, steadfastly she refuses to let one drop of alcohol pass her lips lest she succumb to addiction. I can think of other examples of how my mother fears what may make her stumble.

I feel anger toward my parents, anger at what I see as a cop-out every time problems face them and their children. Let us put it in the hands of the Lord, they say; thereby they seem to be absolving themselves of the responsibility of *understanding* and helping solve the issue. They expend no effort in trying to understand, I think, they just want pat answers from God.

Yet anger does no good. I must bury my resentment against them, I think. I accept the blankets and their smothering comfort. The attendant tucks me in, as my mother tucked me in my pram those many years ago.

Patients lie side by side, lined up on the terrace. It is quiet; no one talks. I relax and drift off. I tell myself that I must draw strength and life from the fresh air of the burgeoning spring, from the green leaves that will soon emerge, just like Hans Castorp in Thomas Mann's *The Magic Mountain*. I let the pale northern sun warm me though it lacks the power of its high-altitude counterpart in the Alps. Unlike Hans Castorp, I need not worry about subtle changes in my temperature or about TB germs in my lungs. My body is well. As I lie there, all wrapped up and protected, I think about the patients at Hans Castorp's Sanatorium. I try to imagine what it would have been like to have tuberculosis when medical treatment was unavailable, to be unsure that one would recover, or to know that one was dying. Sometimes I think dying the easiest of all; gone would be the pain of living.

My mood lightens so slowly that progress is almost indiscernible. Gradually I begin to pay attention to my surroundings. The Sanatorium is pleasant, I realize, nothing like the State Hospital Johs was at and no one here is crazy, just as I am not crazy. Less often now, does my brain send me panic signals, and the oppressive sadness that hovered over me as a black cloud gradually dissipates. The psychiatrist reassures me that I am not about to become schizophrenic.

I now have my meals with the other patients, eating in the large, formal dining room where starched white linen tablecloths cover the tables and where my napkin is folded into a linen pouch. In the pleasant living room, with its comfortable furniture and its French doors opening on to the patio and the park, I eventually accompany singers among the patients on the piano. Before long, I also visit the library and begin reading again.

I am walking in the woods. Anemones spread their carpet of green leaves and delicate white flowers on the forest floor; buds on the trees teeter on the brink of exploding into leaves. Though a recurrent event, the fragrance of beech woods coming alive always catches me off-guard and fills me with surprise and nostalgia. Walking with me is a young man, thickset with blonde, curly hair. He is enamored with me, I know, but I think him slightly boring. A fellow patient, he talks about his travails. Despite his powerful physique, he seems fragile. He is a butcher's apprentice and not at all suited for his job; life constantly fractures him. We spend time with each other because we alone among the patients are young and single, but I think him pretentious, trying to be someone he is not. He writes me poems, bad poems, I think.

"Have you ever read Aksel Sandemose?" he asks me.

"Yes," I say. These days everyone is reading *A Refugee Crosses His Path*. Yet I had not expected him to read it.

"It was a revelation to me to hear Sandemose write about the unspoken laws of Jante," he says. "They apply equally to my home town and, I suspect, to any other place in Denmark. How true they are," he says with bitterness.

Nothing has gripped society in recent years as much as the scathing comments by Aksel Sandemose, a Danish-Norwegian author, on Danish society's crippling proscriptions, The "Jante-laws" Sandemose calls them: Don't think you are special; don't think you are smarter than us; don't think you know more than us; don't think you are more important than us; don't think you are good for anything; don't think anyone cares about you; don't think you can teach us anything.

"That is how people think," the young man says, "those are the messages they give and that is how they keep everyone down."

"You shouldn't care what people think," I say, "just believe in yourself."

Then I wonder what unspoken message I give him—judging him. Oh, please don't let me be like my mother who is so quick to judge people who fail to measure up to her standards. I fear one of my own cardinal sins is my intellectual snobbery.

After three months I am doing well and in the fall of 1957 I return to my studies.

Yes, how well I remember, I think as we drive past the entrance to the Sanatorium. There on the roof-terrace I spent my afternoons watching the clouds and the treetops. What a luxury! I don't know if the Danish medical system of 2002 still allows that kind of care for its populace; I suspect fiscal restraints may have caused some rethinking of nursing patients back to mental health in such a beautiful setting. I speculate, however, that this was a civilized and respectful way of treating broken people. I look towards the beech woods that I had so enjoyed during my many stays in the town of Dianalund and at

Kolonien Filadelfia; the woods stretch north for several kilometers as they had half a century before. Nothing much has changed, although the park looks smaller. Has the widened road encroached upon it? I wonder about my diagnosis. Did I have clinical depression or was it just the mono? Maybe it is irrelevant; I was put back on track here.

As we drive away from Dianalund, bittersweet feelings again fill me: memories of very difficult times in a warm and supportive environment. These are my other roots. My father, Elin, and I had spent formative years here, years that had shaped us.

Hans and I continue on to Copenhagen and catch our early afternoon flight back to the United States.

Struggling

Iceland comes up on the horizon, bathed in sun, and we land there shortly after, a brief stopover before we head towards Minneapolis. The year before we had enjoyed this treeless country that despite its greenness in summer seems barren like the desert. Settlements sprinkle the vast interior of the country like little oases, reminiscent of the upcountry of the Protectorate, but unlike the latter, this northern nation is firmly entrenched in the modern world. Priding itself in its self-sufficiency, it grows bananas in thermally heated greenhouses. Yet, there is a quiet desperation about its people, isolated as they are.

As I settle into the plane for the last leg home, I return to the memory of the Sanatorium, and think of the years that followed. I had struggled to maintain my equilibrium during those first years of medical school. So many things happened that it is a mystery to me now how I was able to stay the course. I think about 1959—so long ago—when once again my life took an unexpected turn, changing my future. At age twenty-two I was forced to take on responsibilities I had not expected to shoulder for another several years.

1959. I ride my bike there. Through the university park, past the old barracks, down, down the hill to the center of town; past the Public Library—where just a short while before I had experienced losing part of my visual field, had become nauseated and assailed by a pounding one-sided headache, my first attack of migraine, yet I didn't know it then—and along the street that covers the river going through town. The weather is getting cooler; it is early October. Now, I am in the modern office building that was my destination and from the fourth-floor waiting room, I catch a glimpse of the harbor.

"What am I doing here?" I think.

Around me women wait, tired and pre-occupied. Teen-agers, young women, older women, all wait to talk to someone who can help and advise them. Puffing on cigarettes, eagerly and nervously, they sit, some cradling babies, others hanging on to baby-lifts wherein are infants sleeping or crying. Others again like me are alone, and aloof. As so often I feel out of place. I don't belong here, I think; I have nothing in common with these women.

As social workers call the waiting women into their offices, others arrive and take their place and the room remains full.

After my stay at the Sanatorium in the spring of '57, I had returned to school in the fall and had kept my goals in mind. Yet the end of the road seemed so far away there was little reality to it and meanwhile I settled into just being a student. Being a student was a way of life: one studied at one's leisure and attended the non-mandatory lectures *ad libitum*. Finances were often not a significant issue, tuition was free, lodging subsidized, and one could get by on little. I liked the dormitory community in which I could participate as much or as little as I chose. Often I felt down. Then I read, often literature unrelated to medicine, books I had never had a chance to read, and listened to music on the radio or to my only two records, Rachmaninov's Second Piano Concerto and Schubert's *Unfinished Symphony*. I listened to them for hours as they lifted me out of the doldrums for a while.

My parents had moved to Jutland with Johs. They had realized they must remain in Denmark to care for him and my father had found a job teaching at a small country school. Though they now lived closer to me, I rarely saw them. I felt little connection to my parents and when I was with them, I avoided talking to them about anything that was important to me. To them everything was black and white. They would not be able to understand my need to lessen the burden of daily living by escaping into books or music.

Neither did I tell them about my work: night call, sitting at patients' bedsides in the dark, checking their pulses, blood pressures, and respiratory rates, worried about, yet anticipating their deaths, unable to do anything for them except help alleviate their suffering. As I sat with them, trusting myself to recognize changes that would signal their inevitable demise, I

wondered what they were thinking—if indeed they were thinking—many
of them were unconscious.

Finally, it is my turn.

"Please sit," the gray haired social worker says, clearing files off a chair.
"I know it is probably hard for you to be here, but I will try to make everything as easy for you as I can. Why don't you tell me a little bit about yourself
and why you are here.

" Oops, here goes," I think, "I guess I'll have to tell things as they are."

The woman scribbles the information as I tell her how I manage.

"No support from home?"

"No."

"And you are here because your are pregnant?"

Just like that the woman says it! I have thought about this every minute of
the day since my doctor confirmed my suspicions. Hans and I have talked
about it, endlessly, yet it is a shock to hear the word spoken so matter-of-
factly by this total stranger. It boxes me in, I think. It places me in the cat-
egory of the women in the waiting room. Doesn't this woman realize I am
not like them?

The social worker calmly and expectantly smiles at me.

"Yes, I am pregnant," I say. It is now official.

"Is the father of the baby a student too?"

"Yes."

I had met Hans seven months before; a friend had brought me as a date to
Hans's birthday party. We had quickly fallen in love and had been dating
steadily since. Hans was two years my junior, also a medical student. Since
Bent, I had met and dated other young men for brief periods. None held my
interest. But Hans was different. He exuded commitment and passion, and
his devotion to me was unwavering. We were very happy together and I had
felt a resurgence of energy and optimism. I trusted him implicitly. We came
from similar backgrounds; we shared professional and life goals.

If only he could be here, I think, but when I had called the Mothers' Help
Offices to make an appointment, they had told me to come alone.

I have never seriously thought about marriage and children. Being married was something that belonged far in the future. Having children belonged somewhere out there as well. I haven't been sure I ever wanted children. How can I possibly take on the responsibility for a child when keeping myself together is hard enough? And marriage! Hans and I have not discussed marriage.

The woman talks about adoption, and about abortion. I know abortion is an option. Yet though I feel I can't possibly carry through with the pregnancy—I would lose the tenuous foothold I now have on life—I don't know if I want it. I have never thought about abortion in personal terms. Being young, pregnant, poor, and unmarried was something that happened to other people and abortion is not a choice I thought I would ever have to face. The social worker elicits from me the history of my depressions and she wonders if I can make it through a pregnancy. She tells me I may want to think about abortion. How can I even consider that? I wish Hans were here with me. I feel terribly confused. How can I possibly make a decision about something that important without talking it over with him? However, this is Mothers' Help and apparently they don't include fathers.

I talk it through with the social worker without coming to any clarification; I am too confused to make a decision.

"If you decide not to consider abortion," the social worker then asks, "do you intend to marry the father of the baby? "

The father of the baby, I think; that's Hans. The woman makes him sound like an abstraction, almost like a non-person.

"I don't know," I say. Neither Hans nor I have thought that far. It is enough to deal with the issue of being pregnant.

I return to my dorm dejected and defeated. My room looks out at the university hospital across the street; it is pleasant and bright, yet I have spent so many unhappy moments here that I feel ambivalent about it. Hans and I are usually together here, rather than in his cluttered rooms, and he is with me now. Marriage and a baby! I think. I am in no state to marry and how could we possibly manage?

I have pulled back the curtains in the dorm room and the afternoon light falls through the balcony door. Hans sits on the green couch, I in the chair by the window. I push back my hair with my hands; holding my head and closing my eyes, I sob quietly.

I wish I could turn the clock back six weeks. I feel so tired; that whole process at Mothers' Help was exhausting. I wish I had not gone there. However, I know I—we—had stuck our heads in the sand up until this moment, trying to pretend the pregnancy did not exist.

"How would I manage, how would we manage? How will we finish school?"

Hans is pacing the floor, wringing his hands.

"I think we could manage. We could marry, have the baby, and still finish school. Others have done it."

Others may have done it, I think, but can we? Though I feel good right now, I worry about being unable to cope if depression hits again. However, maybe that won't happen, maybe marriage to Hans will change all that. I feel a glimmer of hope.

I think he is right. I think that is what we want. I just had not been prepared to make that commitment yet, and I am sure he hadn't either, but I think that maybe everything will be better once we marry.

I feel stronger already; I can tell he does too. We smile at each other. Weak, wistful smiles, but smiles nonetheless.

Yet there are so many unknowns. What is being married all about? And having a baby? We have not even passed the first part of our medical exam. There is no guarantee we will ever become doctors, and if we don't, what then? I find it impossible to think beyond that; there are so many uncertainties.

"We will just take it one day at a time," he says.

"Yes," I say and through my tears, I smile at him.

The baby was born overdue. I looked at his long skinny body. He was beautiful, I decided. His skin was pale, his features so regular and perfect, and his hair thick and dark. He had arrived healthy and vigorous after a long labor with green fluid oozing from me for hours. Later, I, the neonatologist, would know what I didn't know then: Michael had all the features of a post-mature baby, and thankfully none of the attendant problems.

He came to me for nursing, but otherwise the nurses kept him in the nursery. I needed to rest, they told me, but I wished the baby could be with me, we needed to get acquainted. I had hardly ever held an infant, let alone a baby, and I felt awkward and inexperienced.

Throughout the pregnancy, I had felt so calm, happy, and relaxed, nothing rattled me, and during the delivery, I felt wired, high with anticipation. Yet, after Michael was born my spirits plummeted. Not that I doubted my ability to learn how to care for him, not that I questioned my love for him, but I felt I was on a roller-coaster ride and I burst into tears for no reason, it seemed.

Later I was astounded when I contemplated my ignorance about the whole pregnancy and delivery; neither Hans nor I had had any of our clinical courses then; I knew nothing about obstetrics. All I knew was the little the midwife told me on my regular prenatal visits and my few visits to the doctor were no more helpful; it was an era when women were kept uninformed. So after my first bout of tears the nurses realized I needed their help. They were patient with me, showed me how best to nurse the baby, how to fold the diaper around him without using pins, how to dress him. I quickly gained confidence in caring for him. Yet I felt stunned that I was a mother. That I should be a mother at age twenty-three was not part of my plan—if indeed I ever had a plan—and the inexplicable return of deep sadness puzzled me.

Later I decided that the easiest part had been the pregnancy. I had felt so positive and energized. Hans and I studied hard, he at his desk in the bedroom, I in the living room of our small dark apartment.

Then after the baby was born Hans went to England for a month for his dissection course. I worried about being alone with my newborn in our dark tenement building and moved in with my mother; my father had left his teaching post in the countryside the year before and my parents had bought a house in Aarhus. At this time Mum was also alone with Johs, as my father was back in Aden for a short time. My mother enjoyed teaching me how to be a mother. I was grateful to her, yet I continued to keep a wary distance emotionally, not letting her breach my outwardly calm demeanor. It was a relief to have the baby as a buffer between us, a focus outside ourselves that bridged the gap between us. As we fussed over the baby Mum reminisced about how I had brought her happiness when my father was gone those first two years of my life. I reflected ruefully on how the joys I had given my mother were all in the past. My mother showed sorrow and disapproval that I conceived my baby out of wedlock, and I felt the reproach even more because it was silent. My mother was rarely silent. I realized, however, that I had finally become independent of my mother; I didn't feel the need to live up to her expectations. Yet I mourned that our relationship was not close.

With Hans's return from England and with school again in session our days took on predictability. We brought Michael to the daycare center in the morning where he was cared for by a loving trained daycare worker with only three babies in her care; we studied all day, went to lectures, and brought Michael home in late afternoon. Our one bedroom flat was old and had no bathroom, just a toilet on the backstairs. We changed Michael on our bed and bathed him at the sink in the bedroom. We boiled his diapers in soapy water on the gas stove, rinsed them out in the kitchen sink, and hung them outside to dry. The Mother's Help Office had provided us with diapers and baby clothes and had helped us find the excellent day care, which the Department of Social Services paid for.

After we put Michael to bed at night we again studied. We now had a focus—Michael—and we felt compelled to study as hard as we could. If we could not find our place in life, how could we provide a safe and loving environment for him?

However, shortly after Michael was born I again found myself pregnant. We were not ready for another child, how were we ever going to make it with two children? So, when I miscarried we failed to see it as misfortune; we were greatly relieved and thankful.

We decided to sit for the first medical exam when Michael was six months old. The exam was harrowing; we were tested on the entire basic science curriculum over a period of seven weeks. Anatomy became my downfall. It was an oral exam, and each candidate was given only two questions. One of my questions was: describe the course of the acoustic nerve from origin to destination. Because of time constraints, Hans and I had gambled and had not reviewed the Central Nervous System one last time. The demands in anatomy were ridiculous and antiquated. We were required to know practically the entire *Grey's Anatomy* by heart, to know the course and relationships of every single nerve, vein, artery, bone and muscle in the body. I knew all of that, but did not know every detail of the Central Nervous System! I received a negative grade, the grading system going from +16 to –22. A negative grade had such an enormous impact on the average that I could not possibly achieve a passing grade. The same became true for Hans. So here we were—poor, married, and with a baby—having failed our first major medical exam. Never mind that we were in good company. Fifty percent of examinees routinely failed the exam the first time around.

We were devastated.

1961. The weather in February is dreary with rain and fog. I bike from our downtown apartment through gloomy streets to the basement of one of the old buildings at the university hospital. As I park my bike, I contemplate the meeting I will have with the Social Services' psychiatrist. My doctor, an empathetic woman, has referred me here.

My life keeps falling apart, I think, nothing stays on the even and just as I think I have beat the depression for good, things start going downhill again. There is a pattern to it: I do well for a while; I have great energy and hope, I even rebounded after the miscarriage; but now that the failed exam seemingly has dashed all hopes, I can see no way out. Michael is a happy baby who greets us with a bright-eyed smile every morning, yet though I love going to his crib to pick him up, even he cannot cheer me. I wonder if I am doomed to spend my life bouncing back and forth between great ambitions and quashed dreams.

The psychiatrist is a small man with dark hair and a beard. He is very matter-of-fact and I think:

"Maybe my problems are negligible and not worth mentioning. Surely he sees people who are much more devastated than I am. I have been given intelligence and a chance at a good education, and I have squandered it. He will, I am sure, think that I am bringing about my own downfall—repeatedly. He will think me a complainer."

My mother has encouraged me to ask God for help; this might not have happened had I not turned my back on God. She is disappointed, I know; things have not gone for me the way she hoped, but I studiously avoid sharing anything with my mother. Hans and I will manage on our own. I have to hand it to my mother, however. Though she might have preferred that I had waited to marry and have a family until I was done with my studies, she does acknowledge that marriage and responsibilities have been good for me. At least it has me deeply engaged in my studies and my mother more than anything wants to see me become a doctor. Yet I keep my mother at the periphery of my life; I believe neither my mother nor God can help me.

I am gratified to find that the psychiatrist is empathetic and listens with great care as I describe my depression and everything that has been going on in my life.

"Do you realize what you have just told me?" he asks.

"Yes," I say after thinking his question over. "I have told you that I constantly screw up, that I am a whiner, and that it's my own fault that I am unable to succeed at anything. And you are telling me I deserve to feel the way I do?"

"Yes," he said," I think you do deserve to feel the way you do. I cannot imagine how you could feel any other way. But for reasons other than the ones you list. In the past year, you have had one pregnancy and a delivery; then another pregnancy before your body recovered from the first; a miscarriage; and all the while you have been studying day and night, caring for a baby, and never allowing yourself any rest. What do you think you are? Superwoman?" He smiles, and his quiet demeanor softens the intended sting of his question.

"I don't pretend to be superwoman," I say vehemently, "I can't even achieve the least of my goals. Don't make fun of me. I know I am complaining."

"Complaining! You should be complaining much more because I think your body is screaming for you to slow down; it is trying to tell you something. Your body and mind can't keep up with what you are demanding of yourself."

If I weren't so depressed, if I wasn't so disturbed by his comments I would laugh at him. So he thinks I demand too much of myself. My problem is that I demand too little! If I had demanded more, I would have passed that damn exam, we both would have. We could be out of that dump of an apartment we live in; it is so dark the sun never reaches it. He doesn't understand that

I am supposed to be a strong person; I am supposed to be able to handle everything....

"Yes, I am right, you did think you were supposed to be superwoman." He says this with a quiet chuckle. By this time, I am crying, crying tears of frustration. I must get back on track; I must continue to demand more of myself. If I don't, I can never look myself in the eye again. I feel so ashamed that I fail over and over.

Our conversation continues from there. He puts me on a new anti-depressant, which in due course helps me and he has me come back many times to talk to him.

Yet it is not until many years later that I realize he had been right; I had demanded the unreasonable of myself. And I remain indebted to him; he helped me, not just by giving me an anti-depressant that worked reasonably well, but by believing in me. What was more: I had the unfailing support of my husband. Not once did I consider quitting my studies, not once did Hans suggest that I do so. We both accepted living at subsistence level until we both had our degrees.

A year later Hans and I had passed the first of our medical exams with excellent grades. We knew then we were on our way. No one ever failed the second exam. The first exam was the gate keeper, keeping out of the medical profession the ones who had no stamina, the ones who could not assimilate large amounts of information and regurgitate them on cue, the ones who could not muster the mulish, day-in-day-out studying and persistence required. That it probably also kept out a number who might have become caring, compassionate physicians was quite another matter.

Hans and I now had proof we could survive the worst of times, and we felt confident about our future.

Subsequently we finished our clinical years without further ado; while still in school, we had another baby, Peter. We graduated from Medical School at the top of our class, went on to an internship in Kansas City, and later to residencies at the Mayo Clinic.

Though our intentions had been to return to Denmark to practice, our plans were foiled. The Danish medical system did not acknowledge our specialty training and with no regrets, we returned to the U.S. to practice in

Duluth, Minnesota. Here our family thrived, put down new roots, and here we left our mark on the community.

We land in Minneapolis late in the day of July 4, 2002, retrieve our car, and drive north. As we come over Thomson Hill at the western edge of Duluth, we see Lake Superior in front of us. At the waterfront, the fireworks are in progress. It is a spectacularly beautiful evening; we seem surrounded by exploding lights, from Duluth and from Superior in Wisconsin. We hope to get through town before the display is over and people start crowding the freeway.

Driving to our home north of Duluth I think about roots. There they are, hidden, no one paying them attention, yet they influence you in subtle ways every day of your life. Some you can metaphorically unearth and contemplate, others you can physically embrace as we had done on this visit to Denmark, and others are just there, a part of you.

My roots in Yemen, so long buried, have been ever present for the past two years as I have put memories of that time on paper, and now they are constantly on my mind, now that my adopted country is on a collision course with the Arab world. I am convinced a war with Iraq will be a catastrophe.

Now that our life is free of the turmoil that was part of our early life together, we had also hoped that the world in general would have reached a state of tranquility; but not so. Hans and I have talked about how we had never anticipated that the world should be in such turmoil little more than a decade after the conclusion of the Cold War. Foolishly we had viewed that as the end to all conflict and, as many others, we had looked forward to decades of peace and prosperity.

Would we again have to live with the uncertainties of war?

The Thread of Life

In late October 2002, Hans and I are back in Cameroon. On this Sunday afternoon our co-workers from Duluth and we have taken a day off and are on our way south of Ngaoundéré to Ranch de Ngaoundaba. The just subsiding rainy season has turned the road to mud. Foot-deep ruts—caused by over-loaded trucks—and the grader that is now erasing them impede our progress.

At the Ranch I feel back in colonial times. The resort, built in 1962, was intended for hunters from Europe. There is little left to hunt now and the Ranch's twelve rooms are seldom all occupied. We had not called ahead to say we were coming, so for lunch we take what is offered.

We sit on the covered terrace talking, about Africa and about our work at the hospital. An older French man joins us. A mechanic by trade, he helped build the ranch forty years before, and ended up staying on. He now is in charge of the cattle, all 1050 heads of them. The absentee owner, a vintner, lives in France. With ten herders, the old man monitors the food and water intake of the cattle and gives them regular disinfectant baths to protect them against the tsetse fly. He has been married four times, he says, but now lives with a twenty-eight year old Cameroonian university student. "When in Rome, do as the Romans do," he says with a roguish smile.

Our group talks with satisfaction about the workshop we have had for people in management at the hospital. We also talk about a major grant application for a program to prevent transmission of AIDS from mother to child. We have just spent the last several days modifying the proposal. When we first started work here, we focused on medical education and shied away from the AIDS issue: it was a project beyond the scope of our program.

It had, however, become impossible to ignore the enormous needs caused by the AIDS crisis, and we have now immersed ourselves in setting up a manageable AIDS project. We all share our contentment with the progress we see at the hospital.

After lunch, we walk to the nearby crater lake. It is beautiful, and bilharzias free; European guests swim here, but not we. In the lake lives a crocodile, the Lebanese woman Zeena says, a seemingly mythical creature akin to the Loch Ness monster. Back at the main lodge, profusely covered in oleander, we have coffee while in front of us lie the picturesque hibiscus-shaded buckaroos that are the resort's lodgings. We leave the Ranch before dusk.

In Ngaoundéré, Hans and I live in a Norwegian guesthouse, simply and comfortably. The former Mission Station, now belonging to the Cameroonian Lutheran Church, continues to house a number of missionaries. They now work with the Cameroonian Lutheran Church in an advisory capacity; but their community life continues unchanged. Once a week they meet for prayer meetings. Our group attends. As I sit there with old and new friends, I am comforted, and again, I feel as if I am in Aden. I offer prayers of thanksgiving for the progress we have seen at the hospital. Our little group from Duluth has felt privileged to be able to share our knowledge and resources.

It is late the next day. I have been working at my laptop all afternoon, preparing another grant proposal. I am tired. There have been many demands on us during our stay here, yet I also feel at peace. We have accomplished much. I look out across the hills where the local people have started burning off the grasses to allow for new growth when the rains come next spring.

I think of my parents, now long dead. Could they have imagined that I would be in Africa in the autumn of my life? On my first visit here in 1997, a particular event made me think about our up-country trip in Aden with Uncle Raymond in 1951 and how that experience shaped me.

One morning I am seeing patients in the pediatric clinic at the hospital in Ngaoundéré. Patient after patient comes before me. The clinic is crowded, the noise overwhelming, and sometimes I can barely hear the patients' heartbeats or breath sounds. The morning passes swiftly, and toward noon things quiet down.

Suddenly there is a hush in the room. A man and a woman enter carrying a child in their arms. All three have arrived on the back seat of a motorcycle. The father puts the child down on the table before me. I begin to unwrap her and as I do so, my hand brushes the child's arm; it is cool. When I have her uncovered I realize the child is dead. I place my stethoscope on her chest. I hear nothing.

I turn to the parents.

"She is dead," I say.

"'Dead?'" Bewildered and with accusation in their voices, they look at me. "How can she be dead? We just brought her here."

How could they not have known she was dead? Impatience rises within me; why had they not brought her earlier? She must have been dead for some time.

"Can't you do something?" they ask.

I shake my head; conflicting emotions tear at me. I force myself to be gentle with them:

"No, I can't do anything. She is dead."

They are stony-faced. They accept that their daughter is dead, yet they just stand there, not touching each other, not talking. They shed no tears. I know that this is probably not the first child they have lost.

I don't know whether this child's death affects me more than it does them. I want to reach out to them, to hug them, but unarticulated cultural differences separate us. I want to share their grief, but they stand like salt-pillars, grieving inside as they accept death. In my own grief, I also feel anger. I know this child has not just keeled over and died. She has been sick for a while; the parents watched her progress toward her death and yet they did nothing. But I also know—and my anger is directed at the injustices of the world—that the parents did nothing because having her treated cost more than they could afford and meant starvation for the rest of their children. Maybe she would get better on her own, they will have thought, and maybe they even wasted precious time by first bringing her to the medicine man.

Then the parents lean over the child and cover her up. The father takes her in his arms and quietly and stoically, they walk out of the room.

I remember how in 1997 I had thought of that visit to the Clinic in Gi'ar with uncle Raymond where the first little seed was planted in my subconscious, a seed that would eventually lead to my choice of profession. And I am aware of how my first visit to Cameroon closed the circle to my adolescence in Aden. Forty-six years later, I was working in a setting similar to the one in Gi'ar.

How had the visit to the clinic in Gi'ar affected my thirteen-year-old self, awakening as I was to the realization of people's suffering? Until then, my worldview had been shaped, unconsciously I know now, by the whites around me. I had tended to see Arabs as *other*, not *like* whites. The Arabs in the erstwhile Protectorate of Aden had never known anything else, I thought then; therefore, there was no reason to think that they were not content with what they had. My parents had never expressed such sentiments, but in retrospect, I am aware how strongly the colonial atmosphere implied a separation between the two worlds.

Had I at age thirteen been propelled into thinking about the uneven distribution of riches? My family and I had so much more than the people in Gi'ar had. If we got sick we saw a doctor immediately, we would not have to worry about what it cost. We were poor by white people's standards, yet we never went hungry, we had shelter, a comfortable place to sleep, and all the medical care we needed. Yet my young self probably did not know how to integrate what I learned from watching uncle Raymond and I doubt that it caused a paradigm shift in me; the collective worldview was yet too entrenched. Invariably, however, it must have set thoughts in motion, it must have informed my experiences, and helped shape the social consciousness I developed as an adult.

I would have liked to share my Cameroonian experiences with my parents: the continuous lack of resources, the fact that no progress seems to have been made in the developing world, or at least in Africa, in the fifty years separating their experiences in Aden and mine in Cameroon. Despite the enormous industrial and scientific progress that had taken place during my parents' almost one hundred years on earth, little of it had reached the poorest nations of the world. Yet this would not have surprised them. They had seen the developing world continue to lag behind the industrialized world, the gap widening during their lifetime. They would have been distressed, however, by the sharp and growing divide between Muslims and

Christians, and devastated that the pending Iraqi conflict should be viewed by Muslims worldwide as a religious war.

As I ponder the world from my African vantage point, I am happy that my parents who lived into their mid-nineties had left this earth well before the current unrest.

1988. I receive the call one early September morning. His voice is steady.

"Mother died last night. She just slipped away. She had refused to eat and had refused to get out of bed. She continued to lose weight. I knew she didn't want to live anymore. I sat by her holding her hand when she took her last breath."

I am stunned. Neither my father nor I say anything for what seems like minutes. I can tell my father has rehearsed this little speech to keep his emotions under control.

Finally, I say:

"Dad, I will come home for the funeral."

I can't believe my mother died, I think. She was supposed to be around forever.

In the kitchen the sun pours through the gold, red, and yellow leaves of the maple outside the windows. My mother-in-law Fie, who is visiting, has already made coffee. Our twenty-five year old son, Peter, is at the table having breakfast.

Though we enjoy having Fie with us, I wish I could be alone now. But I tell her; full of empathy she folds me in her arms. Hans comes out of the shower.

"Who called?"

I tell him as I try to get myself under control.

"I am OK," I say and smile. "It is not as if it was unexpected. I knew this could happen anytime."

We talk about the arrangements I need to make. I want to go to the funeral. Fie is flying home in a few days. I will arrange to go with her. The timing of my mother's death is perfect, I think ruefully.

Fie was eighty-two then, a widow. She had traveled alone from Denmark to visit us. A terrible mistake, we later realized. Fie didn't remember from one minute to the next. Fortunately our twenty-one year old daughter Christine had met her in New York.

Fie's memory lapses had complicated her stay. Hans, Peter, and I were all working and Christine was back in college. How could we leave Fie alone during the day? Would she find her way home if she went for a walk? Everything went well however, but then we had wondered how we could get her back to Denmark safely. My mother's death solved that problem.

Two days later Fie and I were on our way. Fie was a tiny, dignified, white-haired woman, dressed in a black leather coat, hat and expensive gloves, black purse in hand. She almost disappeared into the airplane seat.

I thought with sadness of Fie's disintegrating memory. She retained her quiet, considerate, loving, and inquisitive personality and I was thankful for that. Yet, I realized that next time I saw her, Fie might recognize neither Hans nor me.

The two days before our departure had been so hectic for me I hadn't had time to think about my grief over my mother's death.

She had been in the nursing home for over three years now. Things had finally gotten so bad that my father could no longer care for her in the apartment. She had fallen several times, she forgot to turn off the stove, had set fire to dish towels, was constantly misplacing things, and was angry and combative. Fortunately, she never ventured outside, but Dad couldn't leave the apartment to shop for food, even though the grocer lived right around the corner. A home-aide came in every day to help him get Mum out of bed, but he had to put her to bed at night. She had been on a waiting list for the nursing home for a long time, though she avowed she would rather die than go there. They had been offered a room on two occasions, but Mum had not been ready. Finally, when once again a room became available, my father accepted. He was worried about her safety and she would get better care at the nursing home than he could now provide. Mum didn't recognize him much of the time. When he told her about the decision, she had been very angry. He didn't care for her anymore, she said. But finally, he was able to make her understand it was for her own good. He would be with her every day.

And so, she had moved to the nursing home. Every day Dad sat with her, read, and sang to her, Arabic hymns in which she joined with a happy smile, her voice now almost in the bass range. Even when she no longer knew who he was, he sat there with her. He talked to her of Aden; the memory of those years was close. Mum had a bright pleasant room facing west, with a small private balcony. She had some furniture from the apartment, pictures of the family, and the wall hanging they had had for years—the one with camels trekking across the desert.

Fie and I make it through Kennedy without problems and are now settling in on the transatlantic flight.

"Wouldn't it be nice to have some red wine with dinner?" Fie says.

Fie had been a gracious hostess in her time. My father-in-law, Richard, had been an architect, and he and Fie had been part of the social elite in their small Danish town. They entertained frequently and lavishly and people had raved about Fie's dinners. Fie enjoys red wine, but her body is now so tiny that she sometimes overestimates how much she could tolerate.

"I think that is a lovely idea," I say.

Why, I think, since my mother no longer recognized me, am I so distraught that she finally has died? For me, my mother's death had been gradual as she slipped into the confusing and alien world of Alzheimer's disease. When I had gone to see her at the nursing home all that was left was her body and her spirit was no longer there.

Yet for me, just smelling my mother's body, touching her fine hair, holding her hand, the right one missing a finger, feeling her thin wrinkled, velvety cheeks, seeing the veins and the spontaneous bruises on her shrinking arms had been consoling. I had savored the comfort of my mother, the comfort I had refused to accept for so many years.

Now there is nothing.

Fie is rummaging in her purse. She can't find her tickets and passport. I remind her that we had agreed it was better I kept both our tickets and passports together in my purse.

Fie pats my hand. "Thank you. I know you take good care of me."

When dinner is served, Fie manages to have two airline bottles of red wine before she falls fast asleep.

I shouldn't be so distraught about my mother's death, I muse. I should feel grateful that I had her for so long. My mother was forty when I was born and had lived to the ripe old age of ninety-three. I had her for fifty-three years, much longer than many people have their parents. But I agonize that I never appreciated her enough. I ponder that there is something almost primal about losing a parent. Most of us go through life relying on our parents being there, and as long as they are, we are their children. Deep down inside we feel like a child when we are with them, as if our childhood stays alive in some recess of us because of them. So when they die, does our childhood die? I wonder. I still have my father, I am still his child, and so I can't answer that.

Fie is awake again:

"I think I would like to have some red wine."

"Fie, you just had two bottles."

"I haven't had any wine yet."

The night is long. If it isn't the tickets, it is a request for the wine that Fie thinks she never had. I love my mother-in-law, she is a beautiful, gracious lady, and I find that I deal with her memory lapses with equanimity. Though Fie has always been like a second mother to me, her mental decline does not distress me the way my own mother's decline did.

There are more people at the funeral than I had expected. If only we could have had an open casket, I think. I would have liked to see my mother's earthly remains once again; but that is not done in Denmark.

After the funeral, there is coffee and cake at the nursing home. Friends and acquaintances give eulogies praising Mum's devotion to spreading the gospel, her tirelessness in going from door to door selling tickets for mission bazaars, and her life's dedication to serving Christ among Muslims. None of the speakers seems to acknowledge how unusual my mother was, and how consistently she defied the expectations placed on women of her generation. Therefore, I get up to talk of Eleanor the pioneer, who blazed a trail to Arabia, who was her husband's working partner, but who also accepted being a single mother when life demanded that of her. I talk about her influence on my own development, how my mother's independent spirit fostered assertiveness and independence in me. In many ways my mother was a much more modern woman than most of her contemporaries, I say.

I rise from the computer and, abandoning the grant proposal, I walk out onto the back porch of our Norwegian guesthouse. My mother seems to be with me in spirit. She would have liked it here. Then I think with sadness that I failed to tell her often enough that I loved her. I never thanked her enough for her love and support, and I never told her enough how much that had meant to me. I sit in a chair watching the hills burn, filled with longing for my parents. If they could have been here, how we would have reminisced!

My father had seemed lost after my mother's death. Though my mother for several years had been off in her own world, though she had been unable to recognize him, he had gladly born that burden as long as he could be with her. Until then, he had remained alert and interested in the outside world, and had continued to live in the apartment, though spending most of his time with Mum. But after she died, it was as if he no longer could bear being alone. Within a short time, he moved to the nursing home to be cared for. He remained active for a while and despite Parkinson's he took daily walks, with Johs as his constant companion. Soon, however, he experienced a mental decline and when I visited him in 1991, he treated me with the polite detachment he might have accorded a stranger. Painfully I acknowledged to myself that he no longer knew me. Though we spent several days talking, I telling him about things I remembered from our shared past, he showing surprise that I—the stranger—should know these things, he steadfastly refused to accept that he had a daughter by the name of Martha, looking baffled when I insisted that I was her. Here was my very familiar father sitting right in front of me, I recognized his every feature, yet he did not recognize me!

Thereafter I heard from Frida and Johs that my father continued to deteriorate and then, like Mum before him, he decided it was time for him to leave this life. He stopped eating and drinking. I was grateful the nursing home did not feel obliged to tube-feed him. They allowed him to die with dignity.

He died on July 7, 1992, ten days before our daughter, Christine's wedding. I did not attend the funeral; I was needed at home. I went through the days of preparing for the wedding thinking of my father's demise and of my daughter's marriage, links between the past and the future, bridges connecting generations.

Beyond the mission compound the fire leaps up the hill with alarming speed; this purposeful putting one-year's growth to rest in the soil, planned when the wind carries away from town, is a death that feeds and gives way to new life, the turbulent and painful transition from one generation to another.

The lingering shadows of late afternoon are suddenly overtaken by the darkness of night. Friends come to the porch of the guesthouse to join us for a glass of wine before dinner. An orange full moon rises from behind the mountain, stark against the black sky. I sit silently, soothed by my friends' talking and by the dark African night.

I continue to feel my parents' presence. They remind me of my past, the life I had with them, and the life they had together; they remind me of the thread of life running through the generations, a thread of common beliefs, values, and desires, a thread holding us together as pearls on a string.

Looking into the future, I see the thread continuing through my children—Michael, Peter, and Christine—and the grandchildren now starting to come of age, and into the beyond.

The author's father, 1958.

The author visiting her father's birthplace, 2002.

A mother and child consult with the author and a nurse (far right) in Cameroon in 1997.